Wear
It Well

Wear
It Well

Reclaim Your Closet and Rediscover the Joy of Getting Dressed

Allison Bornstein

CHRONICLE PRISM

Library of Congress Cataloging-in-Publication Data

Names: Bornstein, Allison, author.
Title: Wear it well : reclaim your closet and rediscover the joy of getting dressed / Allison Bornstein.
Description: San Francisco, California : Chronicle Prism, [2023]
Identifiers: LCCN 2023005763 (print) | LCCN 2023005764 (ebook) | ISBN 9781797221427 (paperback) | ISBN 9781797221434 (ebook)
Subjects: LCSH: Clothing and dress. | Fashion.
Classification: LCC TX340 .B573 2023 (print) | LCC TX340 (ebook) | DDC 646/.3--dc23/eng/20230508
LC record available at https://lccn.loc.gov/2023005763
LC ebook record available at https://lccn.loc.gov/2023005764

Manufactured in China.

Photographs by Jennifer Trahan.

Typesetting by Happenstance Type-O-Rama. Typeset in Futura and Lyon Text.

10 9 8 7 6 5 4 3

Chronicle books and gifts are available at special quantity discounts to corporations, professional associations, literacy programs, and other organizations. For details and discount information, please contact our premiums department at corporatesales@chroniclebooks.com or at 1-800-759-0190.

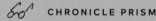 CHRONICLE PRISM

Chronicle Prism is an imprint of Chronicle Books LLC
680 Second Street, San Francisco, California 94107

www.chronicleprism.com

This book is dedicated to my mother and my grandmother. My mom always allowed me to express myself through fashion and never made it seem like there was such a thing as the "wrong" choice when it came to what I wore (although, looking back, it must have been hard to encourage some of those looks). In the same way, my grandmother taught me how to shop. We were always smart and thoughtful, but we also knew when something really spoke to us! We liked to think, but not overthink.

INTRODUCTION

You know how you feel when you're wearing a really good outfit? It doesn't have to be new; it doesn't have to be fancy. It's just an outfit that you know you look good in. You know how you walk a little taller? How you check yourself out in the mirror? How you interact with people differently?

That's because when we look good, we feel good. And when we feel good, we access our confidence. The whole day goes better—a little easier—and those good days stack, along with a sense of happiness from being comfortable in our own skin, which can also extend to those around us. And I love to amplify that sense by making the extra effort from head to toe.

I've been a fashion stylist in New York for thirteen years, but I never really understood what a profound role clothes play in our well-being until the COVID-19 pandemic and subsequent lockdown of 2020. During that time, I had the chance to style over one thousand people from all walks of life via FaceTime. They came in every size, shape, race, career, and from every economic background. I did sessions with new moms who hadn't shopped for themselves in two years and with people who were adapting to an entirely new work-from-home paradigm. (We will dig into both of those topics later.) Some found themselves in the midst of a breakup. Some simply wanted to build self-understanding through their wardrobes—they knew they had cute clothes, but they didn't feel they were expressing themselves fully. (I'll use pseudonyms as I tell you some of these amazing client stories throughout the book.) At the same time, the methods and tools I use with clients—especially my Three-Word Method—took off in a way that I never could have imagined. It blew up on TikTok. *New York Magazine*, *Harper's Bazaar*, and Drew Barrymore all picked up on the trend. Fashion people I had admired since the days when I was an intern at *Teen Vogue*, like Lauren Santo Domingo and Eva Chen, posted about their Three Words. But even more importantly, people who might have doubted their own style began to identify their own likes, dislikes, and desires and learned that once you clarify your feelings around style, you can start to develop and explore it further. I have had the opportunity to meet hundreds of people who have discovered so much about themselves through this process. Working together so intimately with virtual strangers through my FaceTime styling sessions has brought me more satisfaction than I can put into words. It also taught me how little we know about taking proper care of ourselves.

This book is going to change that.

I'm going to teach you how to turn your closet from a place of uncertainty and confusion into one of joy and calm. Together, we'll create a curated wardrobe that makes you look and feel fantastic. We all know what dressing up or dressing down does for your mood. Your Saturday floats by while you wear that cozy jumpsuit, while pulling on a button-down and a pair of smart trousers helps you tune in to your work rhythm. But fashion can only work its magic when we know what we like, when we are in touch with ourselves, and when we bring that self-awareness to our choices, matching our clothes to our mood and even choosing clothes that elevate our mood. Tapping into that power can give you a super-boost.

So, most importantly, I'm going to teach you how to love—rather than dread—the act of getting dressed in the morning.

I can almost hear the skeptics among us thinking: *Yeah, right— you haven't seen my closet.* The thing is, I have seen your closet. In over a decade of work as a stylist, I've seen every kind of closet you can imagine—from a closet full of designer clothes that my client secretly hated to one full of clothes that were two sizes too small and one so disorganized that my client had two of the exact same sweater, and she didn't even realize it. She had forgotten she had the original because it was buried away in the depths, so she'd bought another one.

When it comes down to it, every closet has the same problem: Too often we don't see our closets as the places of creativity and self-expression they should be. Instead, our wardrobes are surrounded by a haze of shame and worry. They're places where we feel we're never enough. But the secret to fixing it is this: In order to create a wardrobe that brings you joy, you must learn to make

friends with your closet. This is the first step in the art of dressing with care and expressing yourself with what you wear.

I was lucky at a very young age to learn to see my closet as an exciting—even exhilarating—place. I had a passion for clothes and a mother who was awesome enough to give me endless space and freedom to experiment with what I wore. My clothes often came right out of a trunk filled with my grandmother's old fur coats, which I paired with frilly princess dresses and party shoes.

As a result, a lot of what I chose was pretty crazy: I was the kind of kid who carried a lacy parasol through a snowstorm. The kind of kid who ran pipe cleaners through her hair to make horizontal braids like Pippi Longstocking. (Not for Halloween, mind you. Just for a normal school day.) I didn't care how I looked— all I knew was how I felt. Which was wonderful. What I wore made me feel great.

When I went to fashion school at the Fashion Institute of Technology in New York, however, I found myself in another league, attending classes with mastermind fashion lovers who were obsessed with how they could manipulate reality through what they wore. They stood out when they went out. I was inspired by their boldness and experimented a lot. Those years summoned all my creativity. I couldn't afford what I wanted to wear, but figuring out how I could dress like Kate Moss on a student's budget—with shoes from Payless, jeans from Zara, and a jacket from the Salvation Army—taught me as much as my classes did about material, proportion, and expressing myself.

Even so, I remember the day I was sent home from a photo shoot for not being dressed right. I was in the early days of my career, freelancing as a styling assistant and trying to get my footing while learning from as many people as possible. I was working as an assistant of an assistant of an assistant and was so excited to be there that I let my enthusiasm shine: tight pleather pants from Trash and Vaudeville, a furry Muppet jacket, and heavy platform sandals. As I arrived for work the lead stylist took one look at me and said, "Go home and change." She wasn't very nice, and while she had a point—jeans and a T-shirt would have been more appropriate for schlepping around garment bags all day—I was lucky. My free-range fashion upbringing allowed me to bounce back and continue expressing myself for years to come. This could have broken me, however, and I've heard so many stories from people who have fielded this kind of criticism and taken it to heart.

We're going to put an end to that.

In this book, you're going to learn to clear away the lingering toxicity and undermining voices that our culture has instilled in us, often since childhood. We've been told that we aren't thin, cool, or young enough to wear what we want to wear. We're conditioned to think that whatever is "flattering"—in other words, whatever makes us look thinnest—is always the best choice. Then there are rules, like not wearing white after Labor Day. I want to give you the tools to see these rules for what they are, and to follow or break them according to what suits your highest expression. You'll learn to reimagine your closet as a space that's yours and yours alone—a sovereign space that makes you feel strong and beautiful, free to play and dream and create.

There is something about taking the time to hear and respond to the internal voices that have kept you from feeling excited about getting dressed—something about looking through a fresh lens and consciously deciding that the critical old voices are no longer welcome in your life—that wipes your mental slate clean and makes a fresh start possible. It's the beginning of dressing for yourself.

From there, we'll get strategic. I'll teach you my AB Closet-Editing System and my Three-Word Method—two systems that I've developed over years of working with my clients to help them really see what is in their wardrobe, allowing them to identify, articulate, and develop a personal style. We rarely think of the clothes we wear as a holistic entity, so these systems are designed to bring your style into alignment, create a wardrobe that makes you feel good, and cultivate the image you want to project into the world, delighting your spirit and reflecting your most authentic self.

I never fail to be amazed by the difference in my clients once I've taught them how to cultivate this love in their own lives. We'll dive into fit and proportion, the basics you can make your own, and how to shop again, armed with a new awareness. You'll tap into your own intuition and learn how to express it.

Fashion has a reputation for being superficial or frivolous. I'm here to show you how to use fashion as a tool for authentic self-discovery and self-care—a practice that will help you better understand who you are, what you love, and how to enjoy it. These tools won't just transform your closet. Little by little, they can transform your life.

I've had the privilege of watching so many of my clients make this change. It's incredible to see someone who starts a styling session by telling me that they hate everything in their wardrobe and are ready to burn it all down go through the process and realize not only that there are some fabulous things in there, but that they have a distinct sense of style. I like to think about the grandma of three who, though she spent all day with the kids, decided that she wanted to feel polished. We found pants comfortable enough to sit and bend in and traded her sneakers for loafers to elevate the look. This changed her feeling not only about her wardrobe, but also about her place in the world. And then there are the closet overhauls that spark a career change.

When you love what you're wearing and how it makes you feel, you're more confident. You move with confidence. You speak with confidence. You see the world as a more friendly place, and, because of that, more possibilities appear open to you. It blows my mind every time. Rather than something we have to do every day, the act of dressing becomes something we allow ourselves to jump into with joy.

part one

When You Look Good, You Feel Good

Why Does My Closet Bum Me Out?

chapter one

While most of us like the idea of looking good—and feeling good—time and again our closets are filled with things that we don't really love. And even with the things we do love, we often have no idea how to wear them. We buy in a rush, we get dressed in a rush, and the result, too often, is that we look and feel . . . rushed. We study images of others whose style we admire and take great pains to dress like them, only to realize that we feel out of sync with our true selves.

This is because we often haven't given ourselves the chance to learn more about who that true self is—and what they really love. And until you learn to start paying attention to who you really are, and what makes you feel good—in a deep down, full-body sort of way—you won't have much going on in the way of personal style.

If your closet bums you out, it's because no one has taught you how to relate to it or how to take proper care of it. That's a bold statement, I know—especially for those of you whose closets are already immaculately organized. But when I talk about care, I'm not talking about tidiness. I'm talking about taking the time to pay attention to your own needs, tastes, and desires—to truly listen to yourself—in a way that enables you to create and maintain a wardrobe that brings you joy. So often our focus is called outwards, beyond ourselves, whether because it's more comfortable to attune ourselves to others or because somewhere down deep we don't fully believe we deserve the time. But when we turn that focus around, towards ourselves, it creates an opportunity to come not only into alignment, but into growth. Small acts that express our nature truthfully create a deeper, more authentic, and more exciting understanding of who we actually are—and that brings new opportunities and perspectives. In other words, if you are ready to be more you, and to find ways that you love to share that, you've come to the right place.

Redefining Self-Care

Before we get to the clothes—what you love, what you can't stand, what you long for, and what's confusing—we're going to begin at the very start. And that means—you! By connecting to our deepest selves and our own authenticity, we access an unshakable foundation that can help support stability in every area of our lives. It's not always easy. Even those among us who have the most loving parents and friends can feel undermined by the ways that the world around us makes us feel incomplete.

Our culture puts out a lot of messages that we internalize: We're not rich enough, not thin enough, not pretty enough, not accomplished enough. It can feel like we're bombarded by the fashion industry, the media, Hollywood, and social media with impossibly photogenic, obsessively styled, and extensively photoshopped images of celebrities and influencers. And even when we like ourselves, there can be a nagging feeling that we're supposed to be someone else or that somehow we need to look another way in order to be truly happy.

Of course, we all know life doesn't work like that. Picture perfect is rarely so. The relentless pursuit of that ideal stops here. I want to support you in loving who you truly are—and to show you how creating and caring for your wardrobe can be one of the best ways to nurture yourself.

This doesn't mean you have to instantly learn acceptance or love everything in your closet as it is right now. Have you ever heard the saying *Your house is a reflection of your mind*? I think the same holds true for closets. If you've come to me for help with your closet, it's because, deep down, you know something's not quite right. Not just with your closet, but with the way you think and feel about yourself and your clothes. Maybe you suspect that it's time to make a shift, to find a different way of being. This holds true for the neatest, most perfectly organized and style-driven among us. I don't care if your immense walk-in closet is as pristine as Rihanna's; if it doesn't fill you with a deep and abiding sense of *yes*, it's not a healthy, supportive place.

Dressing with care is a process and a ritual. It's a way of being that teaches you how to listen to yourself instead of to the toxic cultural voices that are swirling around in your head. So, we're going to start by getting rid of the external voices that haunt your closet—the ones that were never yours in the first place—and reclaim it as a safe space. (This is the part I call "Making Friends with Your Closet.")

I know some of you are probably thinking: *Okay, but the problem here is not with my mind. It's with my wallet. If I had enough money, my closet would be paradise.*

Over the years I've worked with clients from a vast range of economic realities. Money can buy a lot of things, but it cannot buy wellness and it cannot buy style. The only way to cultivate wellness and style is by taking the time to relate with yourself, to notice the things that delight you deeply, and to surround yourself with the pieces that best support the life you want to live. What does that feel like? It's exhilarating. So, while I'm not saying there aren't amazing clothes out there that we all wish we could afford, I am saying that you'll be amazed how many fabulous pieces you find that you can afford once you've gotten a handle on your authentic personal style.

Yet, who we are changes over the course of a lifetime—and one of the most empowering ways to adapt to those changes and to get in touch with yourself is through your wardrobe. During the COVID-19 pandemic, so many people underwent a revolution or a renaissance of reinvention and discovery, sometimes sparked by loss. The majority of my clients are undergoing some form of transformation. While going through their closets may have felt frivolous, especially when compared with everything happening around us during those strange days, that perspective is limited. Through our work, these clients were able to relate to the world, and to their uniquely changing realities, in ways that offered them

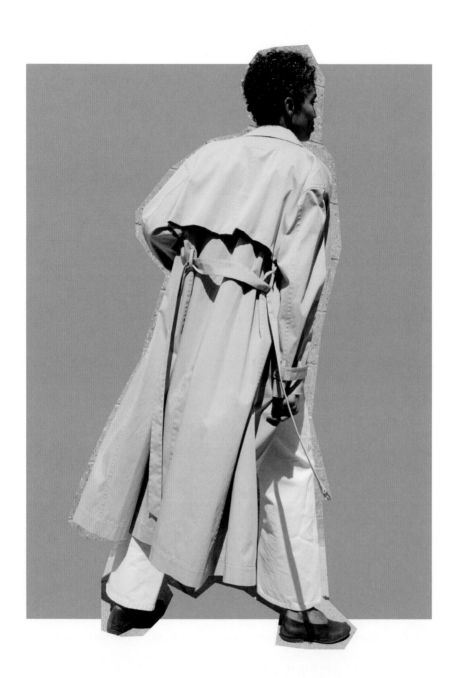

renewed clarity and certainty in unsure times. Going through this process together, knowing themselves more deeply, built resilience and flexibility. As we know, one of the best ways to navigate uncertainty is by grounding into what is true and what matters. You can't transform and grow when you don't know who you are.

One of the most remarkable women I met during that time was Diane, a New Jersey mom with a middle-school-aged son, who had just lost her husband the previous year. Diane was going through a massive shift. She was very petite, but from the way her camera was positioned I could spot several shelves of platform heels behind her. With her lightly tanned skin and long dark hair, she looked a little like Cher, and I loved her from the first minute I saw her. What she wanted, after a year of mourning and taking care of those around her, was to return to herself again. She had a closet full of fun clothes, but she was grabbing for the same few items again and again, and they weren't even the things she particularly liked (a very common tale). She had great jeans in every color—from dark L'Agence skinnies to faded and ripped Zara mom jeans—and none of them were getting worn. Diane was ready to feel excited about dressing, and about her life, again.

That's exactly what you're going to learn how to do. I'm going to teach you how to approach your wardrobe with a couple questions: *What really excites me in here? What feels like the best and truest version of me?* Your answers will provide us with the building blocks for creating a closet you love. (They'll also show us exactly which pieces you need to let go of.)

From there, I'll show you how to bring this same attitude of friendly curiosity to your closet every time you get dressed. You'll be amazed at the changes this new attitude will bring—not just in how you look, but more importantly, in how you feel. And together, we are going to create a wardrobe full of outfits that you love. Even better, if you're consistent about using the methods I teach in this book, I promise they'll bring about incredible changes in your life. There's an old Zen Buddhist saying: *How you do anything is how you do everything.* I have found this to be true in my own life and in the lives of many of my clients. When you learn to care for your closet, you learn to better care for yourself. And that is an incredible feeling.

For Diane, that meant creating new looks for going to her son's baseball games and for running errands around town. A relaxed, go-to look that could also work . . . for virtual dates. I was very excited about the virtual dates, and I could tell she was too.

I walked Diane through my AB Closet-Editing System, a method I've developed to help you approach your wardrobe and learn to dress with care (named after my own initials). Your closet need never bum you out again. More than that, by the time we're done, you'll find it has become your own personal oasis—a place of happiness and safety, clarity and affirmation. A homecoming.

Clearing the Slate

Are you ready? We're about to embark on a very personal journey. It's just you and your closet. The more intuitive and streamlined you make your closet, the quicker you will be able to get dressed in the morning. And the more fun you'll have doing it. This is sacred time: a time for you to get to know and to collaborate with your true self.

If you are someone who switches out their closet seasonally, I recommend doing the system right when you transition from one season to the next. For example, if you are about to pull your sweaters out of storage for the fall, use the system for your summer clothes in your closet first, then put them away for the season. It gives you a fresh feeling and helps illuminate what you have, cutting back on online shopping during those dark winter months when it seems like a good idea to surf sales for a summer look that you may already have.

Banishing the Voices

Before we get started on the actual editing and strategizing, we'll do a little ritual. You'll need a notepad and a pen. (Not your phone; a physical notepad and pen.)

Create total privacy by turning off any phone notifications and closing the door.

Turn down the lights, and light a candle. Don't roll your eyes—this is a ritual, and rituals deserve special care. Only when we begin to think and act in new ways can our space begin to transform.

Open the closet door. Sit down on the bed or in a chair facing your closet, and close your eyes. Let your shoulders soften. We're going to take a minute to hear those negative voices we'd rather not hear—the ones that speak most loudly when we're getting dressed.

Count to ten slowly, inhaling and exhaling deeply with each number. When you get to ten, do the same thing again, this time counting down from ten to one.

Now open your eyes and gaze into your closet. I want you to think about the voices that harass you when you're in there trying to figure out what to wear. I'm talking about the ones that sneer while you're trying to get ready for a job interview, the ones that melt you into a puddle of terror while you're getting dressed for a date.

As they come, go ahead and write down whatever they have to say. Don't overthink it—just look at your closet and let 'em rip. Whatever nasty, cruel thoughts come into your head when you're looking at your closet and what's inside, write them down exactly as they come to you until you have a good list going. When you can't think of any more, when the voices are finally silent, you're done.

Don't fake this part of the process with a sigh and an *oh-come-on-this-is-ridiculous*. Because this slightly uncomfortable reckoning is where most people stop. You need to stay with the discomfort just long enough for the transformation to begin. I'm here with you, and your willingness to be present for this all-important exorcism is what will help it all stick. You will be astonished at how effective bringing these voices out of the closet can be. We're going to track and uncover these voices, relive some not-so-great moments, and then let them go, while we move on.

After all, how many of us remember the unfortunate dressing room comment made by our sibling—or our mom—when we were out shopping as a teenager? Or the unthinking and unasked-for fashion assessment of a certain no-filter colleague, boyfriend, or girlfriend? I think of an old boss who, when I wore a super-cozy cardigan to work one day, asked me, "Are you sick?" She meant it kindly, but I've been aware ever since that styling a cardigan can require a little extra polish. No one wants to look like a grandma with wadded tissues tucked up her sleeves. And then there's our nearly endless fountain of self-generated critique. Just because we don't normally pay attention to the noise doesn't mean it's not there.

Once you've exposed the unwelcome voices, investigate how believing them has affected you. How were you influenced by those voices? How did you behave when you believed them? How did they affect your choices? Trace the thread back and think about the things you say you don't like to wear. Or look at the clothes in your closet that you never wear and think about how some of those pieces ended up in your closet, why you bought them in the first

Here are some of the most common critical "inner voices" I hear from my clients:

1. Hurry! No time to worry about clothes.

2. I don't have enough.

3. Is it cool?

4. It's probably not cool.

5. I can't pull this off.

6. Nothing fits right.

7. What was I thinking?

8. People will laugh at me.

9. Is this flattering?

10. Why does this look different on me than the model?

11. Am I too young for this?

12. Am I too old for this?

13. I hate my closet.

14. I hate my style.

15. What is even the point???

place, and why you don't wear them. Take as much information as you can from the process, which will help illuminate the rest of what we do. Then go ahead and dispose of your list as you see fit. Those words have lost their power. Some clients like to tear up the paper into a hundred tiny pieces over the recycling bin. Some like to run it through a shredder. Some swear by the old-school method, lighting it on fire in the kitchen sink. Whatever route you choose, as you get rid of these voices, I want you to think seriously about releasing and banishing their cruelty from your life. These voices are not yours; they are the voices of a culture that seeks to profit off your fear and insecurity. Cast them off—and, seriously, good riddance.

How to Make Friends with Your Closet

Now, blow out the candle, turn up the lights, and take a seat in front of your closet again. Give it a good long look. That space and everything inside of it is yours. Historically, women especially haven't had much space of our own—and a lot of us still don't. But that closet? It is YOURS. For better or worse, every single item you see is there because you decided to put it there. It's important that you can recognize and own this. You may have inherited some jewelry or clothes that feel sentimental and important to you. The things we wear hold so much power. These items can be nice to keep, but our process is about feeling good. If you don't want to wear these things every day, it is perfectly okay to feel that way.

However—and please, pay attention, because this is equally important—just because everything you see in your closet is yours right now doesn't mean it needs to remain yours forever. Just as we isolated and purged the rude voices from your closet, we're going to purge the clothes that no longer serve you. (And please know that while I use the word *closet* throughout this process, I really mean wherever you keep your clothing.)

The trick is to figure out what belongs and what doesn't. Which things need to come out and which items need to stay in to bring as much joy and ease into your life as possible? Which items make you feel your best? Which make you feel like getting back in bed and climbing under the covers?

Confidence is a special currency, an energy that can infuse the whole day with extra magic when we need it most, whether we have a big meeting on the horizon, or even, as in Diane's case, a virtual first date. Although she was feeling ready to get back out

there, she confessed that the question *But what do I wear?* was one of the big stumbling blocks holding her back. The right clothes can help create a foundation for bringing out our best—the parts of us that we most want to share with the world. Diane wanted to express her fun and fiery side, and it just wasn't coming through in her clothing.

You might think that the first step in reenvisioning your wardrobe is to get forceful—to stand up and seize control of your closet, yanking things off their hangers by the fistful, to decide who you want to be and curate your clothes accordingly. But in my experience, that's actually not the best way to create an authentic wardrobe. In my experience, the best and most important thing to do first is to be gentle. As I've said, think of your closet as a friend. Let yourself get soft and curious about what kind of wardrobe would really delight you. Not the kind of person you think you should be, or the kind of person you think it would be cool to be, or the kind of person you wish you were—just the happiest, best version of YOURSELF. Your soul. Your heart. Your foibles. Your gifts.

This is the self who will show you what your real personal style is. This is the one who knows what you really care about and value. This is the one we want steering this ship. Because when it comes to reenvisioning a wardrobe, the more honest you are about what you really love and how you really like to spend your time, the happier you'll be every time you open that closet door, and the more nourished and cozy and welcome you'll feel spending time there. Your wardrobe can help steer you towards your best life. So, now that you're in this soft, friendly, curious sort of place, look at your clothes and ask yourself: *What are the things I actually wear most?*

The AB Closet-Editing System

The AB Closet-Editing System's step-by-step protocol is one of the primary tools I use in working with clients. We are going to dig in, get real, and focus on you, giving you dedicated time for self-reflection and self-care. I hope you can truly sink in and indulge. There are incredible benefits to be gleaned at every step along the way. Putting in this time now will save you time in the long run. So set aside an uninterrupted hour. You do not want your husband or your girlfriend or your three-year-old with muddy boots walking into the middle of this process.

Step 1: Pull Out the Regulars

Answering the question at the end of the last chapter—*What are the things I actually wear most?*—is the first step in the AB Closet-Editing System. It's the step in which we identify what I call the *Regulars* in your closet. And it's VERY easy. To start, just stand in front of your closet and pull out the things that you wear all the time. Identify all your clothes that are in heavy rotation and lay them on your bed, or hang them on a clothing rack. These are the things you pull on day in and day out, what you grab when it's time to go meet a friend for dinner. Pull all of it out—no exclusions, no cap.

Remember: You're not going for what you like the best or what you wish you wore all the time . . . you're going for what you actually wear all the time. Be real with yourself here. If it's sweatpants, pull those babies out. If it is a million white T-shirts . . . get them out there! Do the same for your shoes, bags, and accessories. We love our best friends because we can be our real selves with them, and this is the time to be your real self with your closet.

Now, once you have all of your Regulars in one place, take a look at what you pulled. What is the common theme? Which

silhouettes do you reach for? Is there a consistent color theme? Are there certain fabrics you gravitate towards? Do you like what you see? Do you dislike it? And why? Figuring out what you are actually wearing is a great indicator of what your authentic style is and how you are currently presenting yourself. When you isolate these pieces from the other things in your closet, the picture begins to come into focus. My client Diane, for example, was living in worn-out black leggings and a big army-style green Madewell jacket. She could start to clearly see that this was more drab than she wanted to be—but it was just the beginning.

If you don't really like what you see, don't fret. With your things hauled out and sprawled around you, you are in a vulnerable place. I've seen tears in my sessions at this point. But all that means is that you haven't given yourself the time to find out what sort of clothes you really love yet—or you haven't let yourself buy them. No worries. We are going to solve that problem.

This does not have to be a messy, overwhelming process. However, I do recommend going through the complete cycle in one swoop. Follow along with all five steps—even vacuum those closet corners and really tidy everything up at the end so you can start fresh tomorrow morning. That said, if you simply don't want to empty everything out of your closet and drawers at once, you can do one category at a time.

If you've made it this far, you're doing great. I'm right here with you.

Now that the Regulars have been pulled together, let's take a look at what is left in your closet.

Step 2: Identify the Nevers

It's time to identify the Nevers. I want you to take everything out of your closet that you never wear and put those pieces in a different area. These can be things that you love but never wear, things that you hate and never wear, things that no longer fit your body, things that no longer fit your lifestyle, things that you don't know how to style, or things that you only know how to style in one specific way. All of these things form your Never pile. When you're done creating it, do the same thing with your accessories. All the shoes and belts and bags you never wear should go in this pile. And heads-up: This pile might look a little disjointed compared to the Regulars. Don't fear, because we are going to break it down even more.

Step 3: Create Three Piles of Never

In this step, we're going to categorize your Nevers into the following three groups.

1. The No, Never Pile

These are the things that you are going to get rid of. They are things that no longer fit, that you do not like, and that no longer serve you or make you feel good. Please remember, getting rid of clothing is okay. Whenever you donate one of your Nevers, you are giving it to someone else to love. It's not serving anyone if it just sits in your closet—and believe me, some of the pieces that you no longer love will make someone else very, very happy. My most recent No, Never was an item that seemed made for me: a Toteme knit jacket that was somewhere between a blazer and a cardigan. The trouble is, when I want a blazer, I put one on, and the same is true when I want a cardigan. I tried it for an experimental FedEx run (tags tucked in) then promptly put it up for sale. Off it went with all my blessings. I love thinking that my mistake will become someone else's great good luck.

You may have outgrown an item emotionally—maybe you're in a different stage of life than when you bought it. You may have outgrown it physically, which happens to everyone. You may have worn it to shreds, and it's just not presentable anymore. But if your closet is stuck in the past, you might find yourself stuck too. Keeping around the things that you no longer need encourages stagnation on every level. If you are holding onto things that represent past versions of yourself or are trying to make things work that you don't really love, you're not allowing yourself to really access who you are and share the best version of yourself. Let those things go.

When gathering up all the Nevers, it's good to have a box, garbage bag, or suitcase that you can just throw all of them into. I find that if I keep looking at the same piece of clothing for too long, I start to doubt myself and often add it back into the mix. I think once you have decided that a piece does not serve you, fit you, or make you feel fabulous, it should go away. Once these pieces are out of sight in a bag or box, you may even feel a wave of relief.

2. The Not Now Pile

These are things that you don't want to get rid of, but you also don't want in your closet. Examples include maternity clothing, clothing for specific events, sentimental items that you don't want to wear but also don't feel comfortable getting rid of, or just things that are simply question marks.

I find that this pile is VERY useful in helping those of us who have a hard time purging. You can put Not Now pieces in a suitcase, box, or separate closet. They should be in a place where you can access them, but not too easily. If three months go by and you haven't reached for a piece or thought about it, then it is time to let it go. Put it in your calendar. I would say that nine out of ten times, the things that go in the Not Now pile end up getting donated. I have one client who donates her Not Now box every time it's filled to the rim.

3. The How Pile

The Hows are the pieces that you love but don't know how to style. These are usually things that you LOVED in the store but that have sat in your closet since. Or they are things that you loved on someone else but aren't sure how to make your own. For Diane, this was a fantastic Veronica Beard houndstooth blazer with shiny gold buttons, and when we tried it over a soft, vintage-looking AC/DC T-shirt and jeans, she was literally jumping for joy.

Allow for an Emotional Override (EO)

As someone who LOVES clothing, I am very familiar with the excited feeling you get when you see an amazing piece that calls out to you. It might not fit with your aesthetic, but something about it begs you to buy it. This is what I call the Emotional Override. These are the pieces that don't necessarily square with the rest of your closet but that leave room for possibility. It is nice to have something that reminds you of a certain time and a certain place, or serves as a North Star guiding you towards how you'd like to evolve your style.

The idea here is to not be too rigid or dogmatic with the EO process—to leave a little room for growth and exploration. For example, I have a pair of bright red Repetto flats that I ADORE. They make no sense with the rest of my wardrobe, which is all based on neutral tones, but something in me delights in them. Maybe they are an arrow pointing towards future growth, or just a reminder of my childhood Pippi Longstocking–self, but I love them. I recommend all readers allow themselves to express a little freedom this way if the opportunity presents itself. You never know where it may lead.

Here are some questions that can help you to gather useful information about your pieces along the way. Ask yourself:

Do I wear this? If yes, it's a Regular. If not, it's probably best categorized in one of the Nevers.

How do I FEEL when I wear this? If it's something you wear all the time but you hate it, that's also important. Even if it's a Regular, let's shift that piece into the No, Never category and look for another version or style that would serve the same purpose.

How do I wear this? If it's something you wear in the same way all the time, it might be a piece you can think about restyling.

Step 4: Celebrate the Revival

Once we've gotten rid of all the Nevers, we're left with the clothes we wear all the time (the Regulars) and the clothes we love but never wear (the Hows). If the Regulars are our "safe space," then the Hows are our wild cards. Our job now is to figure out how we can combine them. For example, let's say you have a lot of jeans and simple blazers in your Regulars that you often wear together, and a funky printed blazer in your Hows. You could try pairing the printed blazer with your jeans in place of your simple blazer. The look would fit with your aesthetic—but still feel a little more interesting. Pairing one of your wild cards with one of your regulars is a way to allow yourself to evolve and take some risks, while still feeling like yourself!

Taking your wardrobe apart and rebuilding it again has huge advantages. During my session with Diane, we worked a lot with proportion. She had great pieces, and her go-to looks, but going through the whole editing process enabled us to integrate

everything she had and loved in a new way that addressed her new needs. She wanted to create a relaxed look for working from home, but because she's just over five feet tall, she was reluctant to give up her wedges, which she usually wore with cropped skinnies. That combination made her legs look shorter, but when she pulled on a pair of flared denim jeans to wear with the wedges, we discovered the new Diane. The high-waisted bells fell just over her big heels to create a long leg. And with her straight Cher-like hair, we were in business. Diane also learned that her beautiful range of printed silk blouses—which she had designated "for work only"—would be just the thing for a date night. This happens so often. When we buy something for work, or for the weekend, we might not realize it can be styled and worn in different ways. While Diane usually paired her blouses with trousers or a blazer for work, when she tried one on with leather leggings, it was a whole different look—both pretty and a little seductive. We chose a slightly sheer Equipment blouse and added a cute black lace bra underneath, just in case. Unbuttoning the top a little more than she would for work gave the illusion of a superlong neckline. We topped it off with a pair of gold hoops, and the result was really stunning.

Step 5: Get Very Organized

Now it's time to organize and reassemble our newly curated closets. I am going to ask you to be very methodical here. I want you to organize your closet by category and color. Take all of the clothes in your Regulars and How piles and divide them up in sections in your closet, so you'll have a blazers section, a blouse section, a pants section, a skirts section, a dresses section, etc. Every category of clothing you have should have its own little section, and within each section, group the pieces that are the same color together.

Take my word on this: It's one of the great pleasures in life to be able to stand in front of your closet, know that it contains only clothes you truly love, and see your things arranged neatly and pleasingly in front of you.

How the AB Closet-Editing System Teaches You to Shop

Now you are organized and armed with a whole lot of new information. You know what you have, what you wear, what you need, and a lot more about what you love. There's so much more to come, but even this alone will help you become a smarter shopper, one who makes much better decisions moving forward. Here is the thing about having a super-organized closet: It actually makes your life SO MUCH EASIER. By organizing your closet by category and color, you get a better view into what you actually have, and this will help enormously in terms of figuring out how to put your clothes together into looks and identifying what you may want to buy the next time you go shopping. If you've found that your new, honed wardrobe has some gaps in it, that's fine. At least now you know where the gaps are and you won't shop for things willy-nilly, buying with no direction. Identifying gaps is key. It can also help you take the curating process one step further. For example, maybe you will realize that you have three blue-and-white striped shirts—do you need all of those? Maybe you could use one more pair of long, dark trousers. Could you sell one of those blue-and-white shirts at a consignment shop and look for a pair of really chic navy trousers while you're there? So take it slow and do not run out to go shopping just yet. Reflection, intention, and strategy will all come into play.

For example, if you just got rid of all your silk camisoles, that does not mean you need new silk camisoles—obviously you weren't wearing them for a reason. But by getting curious, we can discover something else that could serve a similar purpose—like a bodysuit or ribbed tank to wear under blazers. You can ask yourself, *Do I even need something that serves this purpose? What was it about that piece that made me never wear it?* Maybe you discover that what you loved was the silkiness, but you didn't want to wear a strapless bra. So maybe you want a silk tank that can be worn over a bra. Or maybe silk is less easily washable now that you have kids, so you choose a cotton tank instead. These questions and reflections help you make better choices.

Or maybe you have a lot of polka dot blouses in your No, Never pile? Then the next time you go shopping, you know to avoid the polka dot section. Or maybe when you were organizing and sorting your closet, you saw that you had six white long-sleeved T-shirts . . . seems like we're good on those for a while.

So before you go shopping, take a mental snapshot of your newly organized closet. Having a visual helps you understand your style and helps you shop in a way that makes sense for what you wear. For example, if your closet is filled with neutrals and you come across a bright yellow sweater, think about how that sweater will look hanging in your closet. If it sticks out like a sore thumb, maybe that means it won't work with the things that you already have. If, on the other hand, a little voice inside of you pipes up and says, *Ooh! I love that bright yellow with my beige wool trousers. That is exactly what I've been looking for! I'm going to wear it to dinner tomorrow night*, then that's probably a pretty good sign that yellow sweater is a safe bet—and an important key to understanding your personal style. We'll dive deep into shopping later in the book, but I hope you can already sense how what you've accomplished so far is creating some great shifts.

Curating Your Closet

Remember how in the beginning of this process I talked about the idea of your closet as a sovereign space? One in which you and you alone are in charge? Now that we've purged your closet of unwanted voices, cleared out the clothes that no longer serve you, and organized your wardrobe into a symphony of colors, patterns, and orderly sections, I want you to go stand in front of it and see how you feel. Pause and savor. Not only will this new level of organization give you a lovely sense of calm and control, you'll also get the glowing sense of recognition that comes from assembling something that truly reflects your own tastes, needs, and desires.

How does it feel, knowing that everything in that space is something you love? Something that gives you a full-body *yes*? Doesn't it make you feel kind of awesome and regal? Kind of sexy and powerful? Do you find yourself standing up a little taller and prouder at the sight of these clothes that feel so truly yours—at the knowledge that you've taken the time to listen to yourself and notice what truly delights you? To choose those things and present them with care?

Your closet is a "working space," not an archive. That means that it is a sacred space that is always reflecting who we really are—and who we are becoming. If we are moms and our daily life consists of pickup and drop-off, we need to make sure our closets reflect that, and the fact that there's nothing wrong with planning for—and dressing for—these moments. It's good to take care and think about what you wear even when you're just going to pick up

your kids, because these "in between" moments are what make up our lives and our style. We aren't Carrie Bradshaw. Our closet shouldn't be a showroom. We want beauty, but we also want to see ourselves—our true selves—reflected in the space.

You might already have some ideas about where you'd like to take your style from here, which is the subject we'll tackle next. Or maybe you've discovered that you've been trying to express your style all along, but not in an organized way. When Diane and I finished our closet consultation, she said, "I didn't realize how many good clothes I had!" I love that. This process is a chance to reintroduce you to parts of yourself that you've missed. Diane was genuinely excited to start dating again, in part because now she felt truly ready.

Of course your closet is not finished yet; we're just beginning the process of defining and refining your personal style. But isn't it lovely, just coming this far? Doesn't it make you feel right—and well?

Your Closet as a Sanctuary

Having a good relationship with your closet also affects your relationship with your body. When your closet is full of things that you really love to wear, things that fit you well at your current perfect size, you show yourself that you're worthy. I've worked with women who would not allow themselves to purchase the things they wanted unless they had the body that they thought they should have, and in the meantime, they were mostly miserable, with a closet full of placeholder clothes. It's an incredible feeling to give yourself permission to look and feel amazing in the body that you have.

I had a client, Eva, who hated going into her closet because her inspiration factor was at nearly zero. She had just gone through a divorce and was ready to refresh in every way—she was making big life decisions, but her wardrobe had not caught up with her yet.

Eva loved buying and wearing clothes, but she was reaching for the same things over and over again. So we needed to get organized. She lives in New York City, so her closet space was limited, and it was filled to the brim and beyond cluttered, although the rest of her apartment was tidy and organized. Multiple dresses were stacked on one hanger, sometimes with tops thrown in or camis twisted around the neck of the hanger. Four skirts were all clipped together. Because she hated her closet and never wanted to spend time with it, she just grabbed the same things to wear—over and over again. She was too overwhelmed to feel inspired or to explore.

The first thing Eva and I did was organize everything by category and color, while also turning all the hangers in the same direction. (You'd be surprised how much this tiny visual change can do.) As we went, she rediscovered pieces she hadn't seen in ages. We found shoes tucked away on a high, hard-to-access shelf that she had simply forgotten about. (We moved all her shoes to a lower shelf so she could see them easily.) We donated a ton of items, filling up three large black garbage bags. She was nervous that she "wouldn't have anything left to wear." But once we left the bags in the living room and came back to her closet, I challenged her to name ten items that we'd stuffed into the bags. She could barely come up with three. I think having a large quantity of clothes somehow made her feel comforted. But the moment they were gone, she couldn't even remember what they were. The quantity was overwhelming the quality.

You probably bought the things in your closet because you liked them! So if you feel like you hate your closet or hate your clothes, it's most likely because of disorganization or overwhelm. Your closet should stand for tidiness, for care, and as a counterpoint to life's chaos. Naturally you only want things in your closet that belong there. So, first and foremost, you need to clear out anything that isn't serving you or makes you feel unhappy or like you wasted money.

The more inviting and cozy your closet feels, the more time you'll be inclined to spend there, the more inspired you'll feel when you're getting dressed, and the more success you'll have when creating looks.

Wherever possible, optimize for accessibility and visibility. There are ways to do this no matter what kind of space you are working with. I've seen a lot of very unique and interesting closet setups during my many closet tours. I have seen women who have entire rooms dedicated to their clothing and accessories and others (like myself) who have little closet space and make it work with racks. The ones who are most successful maximize their advantages and discourage clutter, first and foremost.

Your Way

Set things up in a way that makes sense and is intuitive to you. Organize by color, as I suggest in Part 1, or by category or style—whatever allows you to easily find what you need and put away each item. I like the idea of organizing clothes and accessories by style and color because that feels easy to me and allows me to be more creative. If your wardrobe looks messy or disjointed or doesn't make sense, it's hard to be inspired. The goal is to make your clothing very accessible, in order to encourage experimentation. So set yourself up for ease wherever possible!

Get the Hang of It

I have a small closet that doesn't accommodate much shelving, so I've adopted the habit of hanging most of my clothes. While this was annoying at first, now I couldn't have it any other way. It allows me to easily see everything together. If you can take in your whole wardrobe at a glance, you can better see it as a holistic thing with coherence, rather than imagining it as a group of separate items.

I even—and especially—like to hang denim: I hang my jeans so I can see both the ankle and the label. I can identify each style in a second without having to unhang them. I also like to hang my belts. Organization shops like the Container Store sell special hangers that do the job wonderfully—the hanger's crossbar is studded with little hooks, one for each belt. When you can see what you have, it encourages you to reach for new pieces.

Sight Lines

When I worked as a styling assistant, one of my favorite tasks was unpacking the trunks from the photo shoot and arranging the shoes. I would display each pair with one shoe facing forward and one facing backward so you could see both angles, and I would arrange them all by color and style. I'm a visual person, so the way that the rack or the shoes looked was always very important in orienting me within what we were doing.

If you have ample storage to display shoes and bags—spread out and enjoy! If you have less space, you have to get more creative. I have some inexpensive little shelves where I can display my shoes on the floor of my closet. Though some people like to use shoeboxes for storage, when they're stashed away it feels like a hassle to unpack them and then they never get worn. Besides, I've lived in small New York City apartments too long—those boxes take up space. Instead, I usually recommend picking up some plastic containers to categorize your items. You could group them by type, labeling each container on the outside ("evening shoes," "sandals," "sneakers," etc.), which makes it easy to pull out the container when needed. I would suggest doing the same with handbags. Let me remind you that you love your wardrobe. Store accordingly. Be mindful with your packing and don't cram things

into the box—leave your bags a little room to breathe. If I'm storing a delicate shoe or bag, I stuff it with tissue paper beforehand and place it in a dust bag before putting it away in the container.

I also like to keep smaller items visible. I love to display sunglasses on a little tray that makes it easier to see and access them all—something else I learned from being on set for photo shoots. And I prefer working with a jewelry box with easy compartments. I think it's romantic to have a little dish with jewelry in it, but practically speaking, the jewelry often gets tangled and you can't see it all. It's best to have things laid out.

Seasonal Switch

It's ideal, if you can, to keep all of your clothes in your closet at once. I think separating pieces by season sometimes limits your creativity. You don't have to think of each item as strictly a winter piece or summer piece! If you need to make room, the next best option would be to store what you aren't wearing in another closet, or to get an extra rolling rack to put in another room so you can still easily access the clothes if you need to. I put my heavy winter coats on a rack and pack my boots into a plastic accessories bin, which I keep in the basement to make room for spring and summer things. I also would suggest that the only reason to shove things into a suitcase for storage is when they are in the Not Now category (see page 51). A suitcase isn't a careful, convenient way to store what you're not wearing.

Care Counts

I also want to encourage you to treat all your clothes kindly. I don't care if it's Hermès or H&M, you should hang clothes, dry-clean what needs to be dry-cleaned, keep your shoes and bags stuffed with tissue paper, and travel with your accessories in dust bags. Use your judgment. If something feels like it would be smooshed easily, stuff it. If not, don't waste! The more carefully you treat your clothes, the more you will want to wear them. If you just throw things into a pile when you get undressed, it makes that piece feel so much less appealing. You want to feel amazing, not like you just grabbed something to wear from a pile on the floor. If a piece wasn't expensive but you treat it well and with care, you will feel special when you wear it.

Quite Steamy

Everyone should invest in a steamer. This can save you the time, money, and hassle of dry-cleaning. Often what's needed to zhoosh something up is just a little burst of steam! It makes everything feel fresh and new—and even freshening up your T-shirts feels great, lending a little crispness to every item. That refreshed look signals to yourself and others that you put in some effort, and that can help you feel really good.

part two

Truly You—Expressing Your Best Self

What If I Don't Have a Personal Style?

chapter four

Let me start by assuring you that you do have a personal style—trust me! And, what's more, after working with hundreds of people, each with their own histories and experiences, I know that your personal style is in your closet. We'll work on further discovering, defining, and refining that style while exploring how to uniquely express it.

In the last chapter we dug deep into your closet to pull out the Regulars and Hows. That exercise should have given you a good sense of what you love to wear. It might not be a fully formed style quite yet, but this mix of realistic clothes and aspirational visions will become foundational as we take our next steps. Think of each item in your closet as a vocabulary word. Your favorite jeans and most chic blazer. Those printed trousers you haven't figured out what to do with yet. The simple slip dress that reminds you of your love of cozy glamour. Together, they will help you build your own style language.

In this section, we'll get into the grammar—the structures and patterns that will help guide your choices, bringing a consistent, coherent look and feel to your style while also allowing you to expand and grow. After all, personal style is just another way to represent the most awesome version of you—the fullest, most authentic version of yourself, encompassing all the parts that you love to share.

When you allow yourself the time to express yourself through your wardrobe, you'll be amazed at the mental shifts that can take place. While playing with style taps into your creativity, it also helps shape your day-to-day perspective, changing the ways you move through the world. Think of how good it feels to wear an outfit you feel confident in—or one that makes you feel spectacular. It can change your mood in profound ways, and, as we all know, your mood colors your day.

We'll start with a meditation to help you tap into your vision of this most radiant version of you, and then we'll dive into the Three-Word Method I use with clients to spark imagination, while supporting your confidence and your daring. This is one of my favorite parts of the thrilling style-ride we've embarked on. Your creativity, your intuition, and your desire all get to join in.

Visioning You: A Meditation

So who exactly is this best self, and how do we meet them? You'll get the most out of your efforts by clearing some space and time to delve into this inquiry, really sinking in and luxuriating in the getting-to-know-you process, like you would when spending time with a friend. Setting aside ten to fifteen minutes will allow this exercise to do magical things.

Stow your phone. Keep a pen and paper handy. Find a comfortable place to sit or to lie down, and get really cozy. You can do this with your eyes closed while waiting for inspiration, or you can doodle, sketch, or journal as you go through the prompts—whatever feels most comfortable for you as you bring awareness to your thoughts and ideas.

Take a few deep and slow breaths to bring you into alignment, focusing on your intention to get in touch with your true style. Draw out your exhales, long and slow. Then, allow yourself to imagine a you, slightly in the future. This isn't you in a decade—it's just a polished up, glowingly confident, wise version of your true self. It's you next week, or tomorrow, having a really great day. Call up that image in your mind's eye and crystalize the details as sharply as you can. And enjoy the feeling of seeing yourself in this way. Drink it in.

So, what's the first thing you notice about them? What are they like? How are they similar to or unlike the current you? Write down any words that come to mind describing this irresistible future you. Are there colors they're drawn to? What kind of energy do they project? Are they revealing something new to you? Ask yourself when the last time was that you showed up in this way, as your true self—confident and shining? What would you love to be seen as? And as you ask yourself that question, remember that you already are that—the question can simply reveal important aspects of you that haven't surfaced lately. Note any similarities or differences between your future self and your current self. If in your current reality your Converse One Stars are trashed, and you notice that future you is wearing a really chic new pair of sneakers, note it down.

When I envision my future self, I see someone confident who feels good in her body, someone empowered to try new things and new silhouettes—even the ones that play up parts of herself that she's not used to showcasing. So, my future self is not afraid of dressing a bit sexier, like pairing a low-cut bodysuit with oversized trousers. While I'm drawn to interesting colors, I don't often stray too far out of my habitual range, but that's not so for my future self—she has some bright things that she likes to mix with her favorite neutrals.

Bringing this vision into high definition helps you get clearer about what you love and crave, and what no longer belongs in your closet. You can use this future you to litmus-test your style choices. When you're shopping, you can ask: *Would future me wear that?* Or, as you edit your box of Not Nows, you can ask: *Would future me finally let go of those overworn, old jeans?* Working with this imagined version of yourself creates a guide for moving forward. It feels good to spend time basking in the presence of who you are and who you are becoming.

The Three-Word Method

As we plunge deeper into your true expression, I want to introduce you to my Three-Word Method, which is designed to help you access, accentuate, and amplify the details of your personal style. I've found that pinpointing a unique Three-Word combination can unlock so many ideas, serving as an evolving reference point that allows you to sketch out the boundaries of your style territory. Aesthetics can be really difficult to describe. I like working with three words, as opposed to two or four, so that we create tension and contrast in a recipe unique to each person.

Whenever clients or followers on social media ask me how to find their style or avoid jumping on trends that just don't work for them, I always direct them to this Three-Word practice. Your Three Words can become a personal mantra. They are something to lean on. If you are willing to put in the time to figure out who you are and what you like—and why—so many new possibilities for expression open to you. When I shared these concepts on social media, I had a great response. People were craving a language that could describe their current style and the style they wanted to create. Additionally, by using celebs as examples, people learned how to see what they liked and could figure out how to apply it to their own wardrobes in a way that felt genuine and unique.

I love using this method with clients like Angela, who felt torn between the different facets of her life. She's in her early forties, petite, and with a beautiful mane of curls. She was working in New York in the finance side of the tech world, but she was also devoted to being active outdoors. She loved riding her bike all over the city. This meant that while she was drawn towards light, frilly dresses, she also had a strong practical bent—whatever she wore needed to be bikeable. Until we walked through the Three-Word Method, however, Angela was having a hard time reconciling these parts of herself, and she often felt like she had two separate wardrobes. One was sporty and casual—her weekend look, straight-leg denim or chinos with a T-shirt and sneakers. The other was her work look, which was more feminine and romantic, leaning towards ruffly necklines and flowy dresses. Every time she opened her closet she felt forced to choose, and when she shopped it was like she was buying things to suit two entirely different and distinct selves.

Getting dressed felt chaotic and overly complicated—and Angela wanted to change the way she felt when she approached getting dressed in the mornings. Maybe that feels true for you too. And that's what we are here to do.

Choosing Your Words

This concise trio will give you a handle on your transformation, reminding you of where you are, what you love, and where you're headed. It confirms your instincts, accompanies your next steps, and keeps you moving in the right direction. There's no wrong way to approach this exercise, so please let it be fun and easy. You can change your words—and they will evolve over time, just as you do. They may come into refined focus over a few weeks after initially choosing them. Be open to what comes today and to how you can continue to grow.

Start by using the word wheel on page 92 to support your exploration. Make a list of words that you're drawn to and ask yourself which are obvious in describing your style and which are appealing, even if they haven't revealed themselves fully in your wardrobe yet. You will start to narrow down your list by deciding which of the words that call to you are candidates for the three categories below. Some people like to doodle as they ponder their options. Some people choose right away; some like to think about it for a week.

Ultimately, however, choosing your words should be done while looking through the things in your closet. We're going to use your narrowed list to find your style—we just need to know how to see it and what to look for.

YOUR FIRST WORD

Your first word is what I'll refer to as your practical word, a word defined by your Regulars. This is where your style is currently. It's your comfort zone, a place where you feel confident and at home. Look through your Regulars. What do you see? Write down words that correspond with your Regulars. What is the through line? What links them together? If you aren't sure, you can photograph your looks for the week—one image a day—then examine their correspondences. What connects the dots and creates your style?

YOUR SECOND WORD

This is where things get truly exciting. Your second word should be something aspirational, a word that guides you directly towards the future we talked about above. It's an inspiring North Star that will propel you forward. If the first word represents your go-tos, the known terrain where you feel more at ease, the second word is a scintillating place where creativity, curiosity, and growth come into play.

Of course, you don't need to choose words based on this method—though I find that some people really like the rule and that it makes the process easier.

Working with Angela, her first two choices were really obvious. One look into her closet and we could see that her first two words—*romantic* and *sporty*—represented the most obvious aspects of her style. When she learned that her weekday and weekend clothes could harmonize, rather than detract from each other, it was like a lightbulb went off. In that moment she realized that instead of keeping her clothes apart, she could let these seeming opposites bleed into one another, creating new looks that would incorporate one element of each. When you stop thinking about your closet as containing separate wardrobes or separate yous and start thinking more about your personal style as something to be reflected in everything you wear (whether you're at work, out at dinner, or biking to your next destination), that's when things open up.

For example, a pretty silk slip dress or a simple cotton dress could be worn with Angela's favorite sneakers, or an Isabel Marant bomber could be paired with a frilly dress. Through mixing and matching, she could make each outfit her own, which is so much more dynamic and satisfying than simply wearing a romantic eyelet blouse with a frilly skirt.

You don't want to look like you bought your outfit right off the mannequin. Your unique style shines through in the ways you mix it up. And your Three Words help you understand more about yourself, and your relationship to the world, as you decide how to style your favorites.

YOUR THIRD WORD

The third word in this equation offers an emotional counterpoint. It describes how you want to feel in your clothes. The word *powerful* might mean colorful for one person and sexy for someone else. The word *sexy* never means exactly the same thing to different people. Choosing this word can feel really good, like something clicking into place. And if it doesn't, that's fine too. Sometimes finding your third word can take a bit of time and tinkering until you get it just right.

For Angela's third word, we looked into her closet and envisioned what would feel both true to her style and exciting, leading her forward. *Elegant* was close, and even *casual* was a contender. Then we examined what she really loved most among her Regulars and we chose the word *classic*. But as a third word, *classic* also helped Angela feel grounded, more pulled together. It was a word that helped her steer clear of what she felt was too trendy—especially in that crucial moment when she was putting together a new look. It was a word that could bring more coherence to her approach, bridging the gap between *romantic* and *sporty*.

Whenever she felt like something was a little off with a certain look, she could check it against her Three Words. If Angela was wearing a slip dress and sneakers topped with a bomber and thought it looked a little too sporty, she could remove the bomber and rely on a classic blazer to cool things down. She could find balance in a look that had veered too far into romantic, like a frilly top and silk skirt, by adding sneakers, a bomber, or an oversized denim shirt. So, *romantic, sporty,* and *classic* became her new style code, which she could use as a checklist when something didn't work. Each look would incorporate a bit of each word, and the sum total would express her brilliance. Ultimately, for Angela, bringing this kind of truth and purpose to her style felt liberating. "I had such an 'aha' moment," she wrote to me after our session. "I see how interesting it is not to keep these themes separate, but to combine them into a unique style."

PUTTING IT TOGETHER

People often choose words that don't "fit" together and that are even opposites! But that's the beauty of it—we're multidimensional beings, and we can be more than one thing at once. Each unique blending of our aspects is exactly what creates personal style. You can be baroque and love things that are embellished and printed and patterned while also feeling drawn to minimalism. That special blend could manifest beautifully by pairing a sleek turtleneck and high-waisted trousers with a vintage velvet embroidered cape, sleek boots, and gold earrings.

As with any tool, there is a way to wield the Three-Word Method so that it's especially effective. The trick is not to look at each item with the expectation that it will tick all three boxes, but to create a cumulative effect in the looks you pull together that holistically generates the energy you'd like to send out into the world. Because true beauty comes not only through the items you choose, but also in the ways that you play them off of one another.

Word Wheel

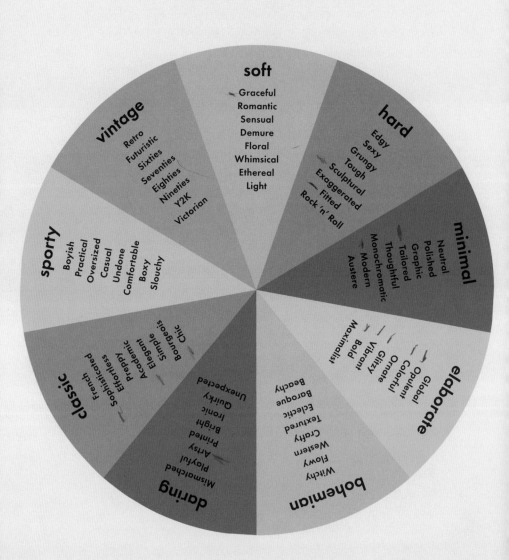

soft
- Graceful
- Romantic
- Sensual
- Demure
- Floral
- Whimsical
- Ethereal
- Light

hard
- Edgy
- Sexy
- Grungy
- Tough
- Sculptural
- Exaggerated
- Fitted
- Rock 'n' Roll

minimal
- Neutral
- Polished
- Graphic
- Tailored
- Thoughtful
- Monochromatic
- Modern
- Austere

elaborate
- Maximalist
- Bold
- Vibrant
- Glitzy
- Colorful
- Ornate
- Opulent
- Global

bohemian
- Beachy
- Baroque
- Eclectic
- Textured
- Crafty
- Western
- Flowy
- Witchy

daring
- Unexpected
- Quirky
- Ironic
- Bright
- Printed
- Artsy
- Playful
- Mismatched

classic
- French
- Sophisticated
- Effortless
- Preppy
- Academic
- Elegant
- Simple
- Bourgeois
- Chic

sporty
- Boyish
- Practical
- Oversized
- Casual
- Undone
- Comfortable
- Boxy
- Slouchy

vintage
- Retro
- Futuristic
- Sixties
- Seventies
- Eighties
- Nineties
- Y2K
- Victorian

The Three Words as an Editing Tool

Another helpful way to use the Three-Word Method is as an editing tool. It gives you a framework that allows you to let go of something that isn't serving you or jiving with your style. It also forces you to look at what you might want to add to your wardrobe in a whole new, much deeper way. When Angela looked at her closet through the Three-Word lens, she could see that she was short on the classic pieces that tied everything together. Instead of guessing about what to add, she could think strategically about the kinds of classics that would optimize her wardrobe.

With her Three Words in mind, she ended up donating a few of her many dresses, which were easy to wear but slightly limiting, as they didn't allow for much innovation. Dresses can be great, but wearing something one-and-done doesn't allow for much mixing and matching. By editing them out, Angela created opportunities to build looks and have more fun with styling. She made room for more classic and versatile pieces that she could wear in a multitude of ways. We found her amazing washable silk pants—suitable for work with a casual T-shirt and blazer, but also great for weekend bike rides. She chose a loafer that was very classic but also played up the sporty/tomboy vibe, which added a handsome edge to the softer looks as needed and provided a dressier alternative to sneakers.

Most importantly, armed with her Three-Word mantra and a new awareness of her own preferences and desires and how she wanted to present herself in the world, Angela also realized that she had choice—power over her message. This felt huge. She could be seen and acknowledged for who she was. She could acknowledge herself more clearly. Using her Three Words as guidance, she could choose to express herself in a way that felt true, intentional, and authentic. No matter what.

We often feel like we need to choose clothes that don't thrill us to dress appropriately for work or for a special event like a wedding. But supported fully by your Three Words, you can show up as yourself. Dressing for special events is a big opportunity to check in with your words. So many times I've seen clients buy something for a specific event, thinking more about the event than about themselves or their longer-term wardrobe needs. While considering your surroundings and cultural expectations is important, you're still allowed to be you—no matter where you're headed. For Angela, I could easily imagine an evening look that would beautifully show off her energetic, romantic nature: a black slip dress like the silk slips she liked to wear in everyday life, with her wild curly hair and a classic red lip. No need to become anyone else.

1970s + Classic + Elegant = Me?

As I get ready for my day, I rely on my Three Words. They're my guiding light. If I had to describe my own personal style in

a nutshell, the three words I'd choose are: *seventies*, *classic*, and *elegant*. I have always gravitated towards the classics, even in my wilder fashion-student years. If I wore vinyl leather pants, I would pair them with a classic mariner stripe shirt and a vintage double-breasted overcoat. These days, I make each classic piece my own through my passion for fun seventies influences. So, if I'm wearing a white T-shirt and jeans, I opt for denim that has a more flared seventies style, or I might add a retro belt. The same holds for my beauty routine. My long hair gives me a sort of seventies look, and I accentuate it by adding mascara to my bottom lashes. That way even if I am wearing a simple black turtleneck and a pair of Levi's, my overall look still has some retro texture and flair.

Over time my third word has morphed and evolved. It's forever a new destination, a new direction I want to travel in. It's important to leave yourself room to explore and be creative. Because I'm generally pretty casual in what I wear, it's exciting for me to think about incorporating more elegant and sophisticated silhouettes. In the past, my third word has been *tailored* because I resonated with the sharp shoulders and crisp pleats of tailored suiting, which brought definition and a traditional edge to what I was wearing. Recently my third word became *elegant*. I keep all my seventies flourishes balanced with a strong countershot of grown-up, elegant sophistication. If I go for a really flowy seventies-style dress, for example, I might choose to buy it in a solid color or a silk texture.

Rules and Breaking Them

Still, my personal style is not limited to my Three Words. At all. And yours won't be either. Your Three Words create way-finding points to navigate by—something to help get you moving. They're a way for anyone who wants to use fashion as a tool for authentic self-expression to first locate themselves within the larger traditions of style.

Once you've done that, you can start to look at and think about all the ways in which your unique style is more than—and different from—the specific words you've chosen. It's kind of like that old adage: You have to know the rules before you can break them. When it comes to fashion, you have to know your Three Words before you can find out what else your personal style encompasses.

Remember—the framework is here to guide you, not to bind you or to force you into a rigid box that constricts your free expression. Lean into your Three Words when you feel overwhelmed or uninspired, and break out when you need a breath of fresh air. And for anyone who has gotten stuck along the way—and this can happen, for sure—I'll share some of my favorite tips for navigating common roadblocks.

"HOW DO I PICK JUST THREE?"

You're not alone! I've had plenty of clients who weren't able to narrow it down at first—that's totally fine. However, the closer you can get to three, the easier and clearer things become, because that succinct trio truly will help refine your style. Keeping it simple, and not going for too many words, supports your focused and edited approach. Still, if the idea of a triad feels sticky, then I've also had clients gravitate towards word pairs or combinations like *French girl meets American classics* or *Anine Bing rock-and-roll style mixed with The Row*. A lot of people pick high-end designers to give themselves something to steer towards as inspiration. That doesn't mean that's what they're wearing, only that it's what they love. So they might gravitate towards Anine Bing's rock-and-roll vibe and the minimal austerity of The Row, but they might be wearing things from vintage shops and less expensive brands.

"WHAT IF I DON'T RELATE TO ANY OF THEM?"

I get it.

ASK A FRIEND

If you feel stuck, it can be super fun to do this exercise with a friend. You can choose words for each other, or you can ask for help narrowing down a wide selection of words. Sometimes we aren't able to see ourselves clearly or we are way too hard on ourselves, in a way that we would never be hard on a friend. So, call a friend and ask them how they would describe your style. And then ask yourself how you feel about the words they use. We're so used to our own wardrobe and seeing our own selves in the mirror that we can lose track of the impact we make out in the world. Seeing yourself through the eyes of somebody who knows and loves you can be illuminating.

Divine Inspiration

Sometimes it's hard to see ourselves clearly. If you need a little support while coming up with your Three Words, you can lean on your favorite style icons. What makes their style unique? Just like yours, it's a combination. When a client is feeling adrift with the Three-Word Method, I'll ask whose style they love or whose style they relate to best, and then together we pick that person's Three Words. While someone else's entire Three-Word combination might not fit for you precisely, their words can be used as inspiration—something close enough to get you started. By breaking down and deconstructing someone else's signature style, you can learn more about which parts you relate to and which parts might best describe your own wardrobe.

Here are a few combinations to get you rolling.

JANE BIRKIN
tomboy, sexy, casual

YOKO ONO
tailored, playful, artsy

SOFIA COPPOLA
sophisticated, classic, thoughtful

KIM KARDASHIAN
exaggerated, fitted, sculptural

PRINCESS DIANA
sporty, demure, opulent

KATE MOSS
undone, sleek, vintage

JIMI HENDRIX
ornate, daring, bohemian

RIHANNA
sexy, tough, sporty

MICHELLE OBAMA
bold, daring, polished

HARRY STYLES
seventies, textured, tailored

ZENDAYA
polished, graphic, daring

"WHAT IF I LOVE SOMETHING THAT FALLS OUTSIDE OF MY THREE WORDS?"

Say your three words are *seventies*, *hard*, and *romantic*, but you find yourself smitten with a stark white minimalistic sheath dress. It's important to remember the Three Words aren't about critically judging each piece but rather about integrating and styling the things you love—no matter what. While that amazing minimal sheath might not seem to fit your words at first, it can be worn under a leather jacket or with a tough boot and can go from feeling like The Row to Saint Laurent. The beauty is in how you wear it. Sometimes a simple gesture, like tucking in a shirt or rolling up its sleeves, can make a garment feel totally different and infuse it with your essence. (More on that in Part 3.)

The Joy of Pictures

If you haven't worked with your wardrobe in this way before, the Three-Word exercise might feel overwhelming. But don't worry—a few steps can ease the transition. It can be challenging to see your own style through your actual clothing. Instead, you might start with what you like by creating a mood board or taking screenshots of things that you like on your phone, including colors, silhouettes, full looks, or specific pieces. See which words describe those things best. What do they have in common? Nine times out of ten, there's a through line. You might see some boho elements mixed with elegant photos of nineties supermodels as well as casual street-style references. Whatever you like will probably be a mash-up of things that you're drawn to instead of just one thing.

Even if your closet doesn't reflect these words precisely yet, you'll get there. So don't freak out and throw everything away! Once you find three words you can relate to, those that feel authentic to you, go back to your closet and see if you have anything that could be described with those words. I bet you do. And even if you don't see it at first glance, you can create the mood with styling. If your closet looks casual but you're aiming for elegant, you might choose to add a few key pieces that will allow you to move in that direction—a new shoe you can pair with jeans and a T-shirt to elevate the look, or a super-sleek long jacket that you can wear with a sweater and sneakers to create a more elegant vibe.

The place where inspiration and lifestyle meet can be an especially thrilling junction, a place for discovering new ways to guide your style. When I work with clients, their Pinterest selections show me what they are drawn to and where they'd like to venture next. Often we find an overarching theme hidden—or not so hidden—among the images, and you may discover this too. For example, is there a color that's present throughout your selections? Or a specific silhouette? Maybe you're drawn to fitted tops and wider bottoms, or the reverse.

It's useful when you're building your own expression to gather images that you love—the ones that give you a huge *yes*, which means they are super-potent and working some magic on your behalf. Never hold back when you are gathering images that move you. Cast a wide net—throw some beauty images or interiors into the mix and create a holistic mood. Images are pure information, allowing you to take a step back from your closet to see what resonates with you. How is what you see in your favorite images reflected in your wardrobe? Maybe the pictures you choose feature wide-leg denim and you are only working with skinnies. Or maybe you notice that every image you pull is popping with color and you're wearing a lot of neutrals lately.

When you see an image of someone whose style thrills you, ask yourself, *What about this person's look would I do differently?* Look closely. Is there anything you don't quite love? These details are worth paying attention to as well, as they can help point you towards your very own original signature look. Maybe you pulled a photo of a great look, but the woman is wearing heels and you are a flats girl. That detail can help you translate the image into your own language. You don't want to copy and paste. You want to twist it and make it yours.

TIDY TREASURE

You will want to organize all these photographic treasures, creating a sense of ease, not confusion, which will help you stay focused. You could organize your images on separate Pinterest boards or in folders on your phone. You could create a folder for your Three Words, solidifying and deep-diving into the energies that inspire you most. Or you could set up a series of folders by item—say, one folder for blazers and another for denim.

Alternatively, you could categorize your images either by occasion or by season. That doesn't mean you can't be inspired by any look in any season, but it allows you to be a little more precise and strategic. I have a folder called *Spring* that I've kept on my phone for over five years. I add to and delete from it constantly. Plenty of the photos stay the same, like one of Uma Thurman in a

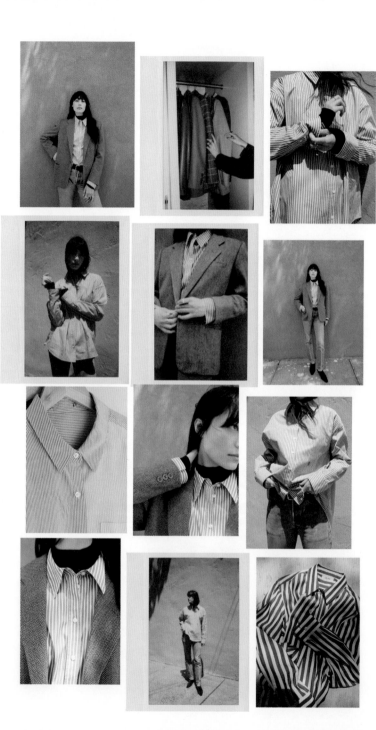

denim jacket and jeans, or Jane Birkin in an all-white look with a black blazer, or even Rod Stewart wearing a leopard suit. But my relationship to those images consistently changes, based on what's going on in my life. In years past, the Spring folder included loads of dressy photos, but now those high heels and fancy daytime looks feel less relevant. Style evolves in subtle ways. A few years ago I might have worn the full Rod Stewart spotted suit. Now I would pair the leopard pants with a black turtleneck and sleek boots or put on the leopard blazer with a white T-shirt and jeans.

Approach your photos as you would your actual closet—you don't want to start from scratch and create a whole new wardrobe every season. You want to add to and edit what you already own. I refer to these images whenever I'm feeling dull or need to remind myself about what aspects of style I'm excited to explore. It's easy to get sidetracked by what friends are wearing or what you see on social media, and spending time focusing on your own sources of inspiration will help guide you back to yourself.

At times, looking at photoshopped, picture-perfect images can make us feel a little heavy. Please remember that you've gathered these images to inspire you and to be of service to you. You're in charge, not the other way around. Bring a positive mindset to what you see. And, in fact, if you see an image and immediately think that your closet doesn't measure up, I challenge you to re-create the feeling or the vibe of the look using what you have. You might not arrive at an identical look—thankfully!—but you'll come up with something that's better, because it's yours. Saving and curating images that inspire you is a way of reclaiming your power around your style and how you want to be perceived, but also how you absorb and process media and your feelings about people's appearances.

part three

Building Your Wellness Wardrobe

What Do
I Wear?

chapter seven

Now that you've taken an in-depth look at your own style and have brought imagination and inspiration to bear in your investigation of what you love, it's time to get real about facing a fresh you. As you experiment with new styles and start to create new looks, it's important to give yourself the kind support that you'd offer to a good friend whom you love. And that means it's time to practice seeing yourself in a new way.

Let's start by acknowledging that when you look in the mirror, sure, there may be some things you don't really want to see. And yes— not every style works for every body type. But instead of focusing solely on perceived shortcomings like "too petite," "too tall," "too large," or "too curvy," when you stand in front of the mirror, give yourself some grace, just as you would when spending time with a dear friend.

When I work with clients, this is a crucial moment, a time to stay open. Judgments may arise, but you can choose to let them sail on by. Just as we did when clearing negative voices from the closet in Part 1, we need to pay less attention to the voices that hold us back than to the ones encouraging us to express, enjoy, and expand.

Each one of my many clients—no matter what their size, shape, or age—has something they don't like about their bodies. And so do I. It's completely normal! And it's not a problem as long as you don't buy into those thoughts. Acknowledging the negative voices while steering towards the positive keeps us available to inspiration. One of my clients was very attached to her story of high hips. She told me that she couldn't wear many silhouettes because she had high hips. I had a hard time seeing what she meant— they didn't look so high to me. Yet no matter what I suggested, she would tell me that it wouldn't work with her high hips. Her insistence that her hips were high was limiting her willingness to explore. Finally, however, I convinced her to try on some things— and she was happily surprised. She had been so entangled with her story that she had refused to imagine any happy ending for herself. Staying open to new ideas means taking a hard pass on negativity.

Mirror Mindset

The mirror mindset is about approaching your self-image with curiosity and kindness. Many of us begin and end our days in front of a mirror, which presents a huge opportunity for framing how we feel for all those hours in between. The morning is a great time to focus on intention— how you'd love to feel. In the evening, you can take a breath or two and use your awareness to wind down, giving yourself a chance to let go of the day. How you see yourself matters. Your self-perception guides what you think is possible and what you decide to pursue. When you feel confident, your options expand. So creating an environment where you can benefit from your own goodwill is a great practice.

Here are some of my favorite tips to help you see yourself in the mirror with the same soft curiosity you brought to viewing your closet. (And if you don't own a full-length mirror, now is the time to get one. You will want to see your looks from head to toe.)

TAKE YOUR TIME

When you try on clothes, whatever you try, don't just throw it on and then say, "I hate it!" This is why I like online shopping and trying on clothes at home—you're in a comfortable space to go slowly. Wear whatever you're trying for a few minutes. Roll up the sleeves. Try it with different shoes. Try it tucked in or untucked. Give yourself a chance to really see what you're looking at.

EASE OFF THE PRESSURE

Be kind to yourself. Too often we're convinced a new purchase will change our lives. While clothes that you love can make you feel great, they can't rise to that challenge, and you can end up feeling disappointed and discouraged.

MOOD MATTERS

Try on clothes when you're in a good headspace. If you're at home, try on clothes after you've taken your shower or put on makeup. Don't try things on when you don't feel good—you probably won't like what you see. If I have my period, I know it's not a day for trying on clothes. Give yourself the benefits of a good emotional setting.

BE KIND

Working in a fancy denim shop in high school, I learned all about the vulnerability and kindness required to shape your personal style. It was a place that carried all the cool brands of the era, like 7 For All Mankind, Miss Sixty, and True Religion, and I learned—through my mistakes—to always give people multiple sizes when they were trying on clothes and to give them time. I learned not to pressure people to come out and show me how the clothes looked. But when they did ask me for my opinion, I was always honest—which backfired when I told someone that the jeans she was trying on were too expensive and that she should wait for a sale—oops! If you can bring this cooperative, delicate approach to your own time in the mirror, it will make all the difference.

SIZING IS ARBITRARY

Keep in mind that while sizing offers a general set of guidelines, it's far from universal and often changes between brands. I had a client who told me that if she tried an item in "her size" and it didn't fit, she just assumed it wasn't right for her. She was rigid about the concept, and it didn't occur to her that if something didn't fit she could simply go up or down a size. It's also important to remember that tailoring can work wonders to help you find a way to customize any piece just for you, especially if you truly are stuck between sizes. A bit of investment could mean that you end up with a great piece that you are thrilled to wear for years to come.

I've also seen how damaging shopping for "goal weight" clothes can be for your morale. It's really unfair to yourself to buy something that you will only wear at your thinnest or to believe that you only deserve to have nice things when you are a certain size. You deserve to feel and look great at all times.

And, of course, it really doesn't matter. You are the only person who will know what size your clothes are—the tag is on the inside. Squeezing into something that doesn't fit is uncomfortable and, ultimately, not worth it. Going up a size doesn't need to cause concern. I had another client who had accumulated a whole lot of clothes that were the "right" size, but they didn't fit. We hung an empty cloth bag on her closet doorknob. Every time she tried something that didn't fit, into the bag it went. That way she didn't have to purge her whole closet at once, but she could slowly weed out the things that didn't work. Without them in her closet, getting dressed was easier—and less stressful—and eventually she loved that the things that remained fit, regardless of the number on the tag.

While I love helping people discover all the gems that are already in their wardrobes, now that we've done the heavy lifting, gotten in touch with our stylish souls, and learned that the mirror is not a mortal enemy, one of the most fun parts of this process is getting down to creating your own personal Lookbook, filled with combinations that are new, that are truly you, and that get you excited about your clothes—and your life.

The Nine Universal Pieces

Although the idea that nine universal wardrobe staples could also feel truly and deeply *you* might seem counterintuitive, the super-versatile pieces I'll introduce below will earn their place in your closet, amplifying your ability to express yourself. You will be surprised. Working with simple, classic pieces creates a blank canvas for your genius. How you wear each—layered, styled, and transformed by your favorite accessories—shows off your uniqueness and makes you feel just right in a way that is genuine. You never want to sacrifice authenticity for style, so exercising your patience is essential as you use your eye and your intuition to find the perfect variations on these classics—the ones that truly suit you.

I can recall plenty of instances where I chose to wear something because it projected who I wanted to be, not who I actually was. Even if it looked fine, it didn't feel right, because I couldn't sense my own authenticity.

These universal pieces are universal for a reason. They're staples for everyone's closet. Like pantry staples, they're great to have on hand because they make it easier to pull together looks that let your personal style shine. If you have these nine items in your closet, you'll always be able to dress for work, weekends, or dinners with friends. I don't think there is a capsule that works for everyone or that there are must-haves that should be in every person's wardrobe. But I do think that the silhouettes we'll dive into here are the building blocks of a functional, versatile wardrobe.

Your Three Words will help guide you all along the way, though it might take a little time and experimentation to work out the combinations that you love best. For example, I always thought I needed a white button-down shirt because it's forever the foundation of every capsule wardrobe list. Eventually, I caved in and bought one, even though it was a little too austere, and it didn't really work with a larger chest. And there it hung in my closet with its tags on. For quite a while. Each time it caught my eye, I felt annoyed and defeated. If a white button-down was supposed to be so universal, why didn't it work for me? It took me some time to realize that perhaps the shirt's crispness wasn't exactly right for me. I wanted something more easy, more flowy. So when I tried a white button-down in linen, I was thrilled. It all made sense. So please be patient in finding your way, turning to variations wherever necessary.

While choosing your perfect version is important, styling is the other key to making these classics your own. To use another button-down example, like so many other women, I have a blue-and-white striped button-down in my closet. But I've learned to wear it in a way that gives it my own spin. While I might wear mine tucked into Levi's with a blazer and gold jewelry, Sofia Coppola might wear hers with trousers and ballet flats. Phoebe Philo might wear hers oversized and untucked. And Kim Kardashian might wear hers over a sleek catsuit. This striped shirt can work for each of us, but how we each make it sing is where our Three Words come into play—and where style is created.

Piece by Piece: Getting Strategic with Your Wardrobe

Here are the pieces that belong in your wardrobe, the basics that can become so much more when you exercise your style, and nine styling ideas for each, including how these pieces work within the frame of some favorite Three-Word combos. You'll be friends for life.

1. The White T-Shirt

Utter simplicity and a breezy equalizer. The white T-shirt can harmonize with any of your Three Words. The white T-shirt is the ideal base, bringing a cool casualness to any look. Use the tee as an antidote whenever a look feels too fancy. There's no single T-shirt style that works for all body types. You may have to go through some duds before you find your T-shirt soulmate. Think of it as a quest. Some people like a vintage look, which is a bit more sheer, while others want something classic and sporty in thicker cotton. If you prefer to wear things closer to the body, try a T-shirt bodysuit. And if white doesn't work for your skin tone, try ivory or cream, or go for a gray or black T-shirt—these are also great.

1. Style a white tee on its own with some necklaces for a clean and simple look.

2. Use a white tee as a layering piece under a crewneck sweater, a very small addition that will give your look a little depth and dimension.

3. Use a white tee to add a casual element with a luxe silk skirt or pants. The combo of the cotton with the flowy silk creates a relaxed and wearable contrast with dressier pieces.

4. **CLASSIC. SPORTY. EDGY:** Try a white tee with leather trousers, sneakers, and an oversized denim jacket.

5. **BOHO. VIBRANT. PLAYFUL:** Style your white T-shirt with a colorful pleated skirt, a flat sandal, and a crossbody bag. Roll the sleeves to give it a more lived-in look, and give it a front tuck.

6. **MODERN. OVERSIZED. SEXY:** Go for a fitted white tee paired with an oversized blazer and sleek fitted pants.

7. **LAUREN HUTTON** would wear her white tee fitted with trousers, a menswear-inspired black leather belt, and loafers.

8. **ZOË KRAVITZ** would pair a thicker, oversized white tee with slouchy trousers, and she'd elevate the look with chunky gold hoops and loafers.

9. **KATE MOSS** would pair a vintage, thin T-shirt with black slim jeans, boots, and a vintage military jacket.

2. The Button-Down Shirt

Whether in denim, blue-and-white stripes, or classic white, the button-down is a staple that belongs in every wardrobe—including yours. I love the button-down's iconic elegance and subversive versatility. It's the ultimate layering piece.

CHOOSING YOUR BUTTON-DOWN

Look for something timeless and classic, if that feels genuine to you. And, conversely, if the traditional button-down is a little too minimal, try something with a Peter Pan collar, a ruffle at the sleeve, or even something that ties at the neck. If cotton isn't your jam, go for silk or satin. They can be styled the same way. Since I love a seventies vibe, a vintage-looking Western denim shirt is a staple for me. Whatever you choose, rolling the sleeves is crucial. A button-down needs your zhoosh to keep it from looking boxy and impersonal. Rolling the sleeves, or simply pushing them up, makes all the difference.

1. Unbutton it slightly, showing off some layered necklaces. Or wear it even more unbuttoned, showing a bit of a lacy bra.

2. Wear it open over a T-shirt or open over a fitted tank or bodysuit, giving you a little coverage and introducing a menswear element to your look.

3. Pack one when you go on vacation to wear as a shirt, a jacket, or a great cover-up at the beach.

4. **EIGHTIES. SPORTY. CASUAL:** Try an oversized cotton button-down with a pair of high-waisted trousers. Tucking in the big shirt feels kind of retro in a great way. I would top it off with a pair of sneakers and a crossbody bag. Or you can go a little sportier with cycling shorts, white socks, and sneakers.

5. **QUIRKY. ARTSY. COLORFUL:** Go for a solid-color cotton shirt in a fun color like orange or green. Pair it with printed pants and wear it untucked to create a funky proportion.

6. **CASUAL. OVERSIZED. TEXTURED:** Try an oversized linen button-down open over a ribbed tank. This has great texture play while still feeling super casual and easy.

7. **HARRY STYLES** would wear a printed silk button-down with some flared pants.

8. **KATE MIDDLETON** would wear a classic blue-and-white striped button-down under a navy sweater with a pair of slim-leg jeans and ballet flats. Preppy, casual, and smart.

9. **SADÉ** would wear a denim button-down with jeans, gold hoops, and a red lip.

Show Them You Care

So many of your Universal wardrobe items are also investment pieces, not in that they have to be expensive, but in that they are the kinds of clothes that—if you take good care of them—can last for a long, long time.

Dry-clean, steam, and lint-roll your blazers. I don't take mine to the dry-cleaner too often, but I pamper them with a little neatening up as needed.

Denim doesn't need washing after every wear. Typically wash jeans on cold, then hang to dry. Only throw denim in the dryer when you want to shrink them up a bit.

Buy a fabric stone or lint shaver to preserve your sweaters. These tools help you remove the pills and make your knits feel fresh.

It's worth the effort to use boot-shapers to keep your higher boots from aging in your closet. I just started doing this and it makes a huge difference.

Take shoes to the cobbler before you even wear them and have rubber soles added if they are shoes you'll walk in often.

Clothes and shoes are meant to be worn and loved and used, but the better you treat them, the more you will value them—and the better you'll feel when you get dressed.

3. The Black Turtleneck

People assume that a black turtleneck can't be cool. But you can turn this base layer into anything you want it to be—it's all in the styling. Look at photos of any fashion icon dressed in a sleek and chic black turtleneck—Marilyn Monroe, Steve Jobs, and Janet Jackson, to name a few. No matter what the decade, each image still feels fresh and modern. Ask yourself how you'll wear it most—on its own or as a layer? If it's something you will layer with, then go for a thin and comfortable turtleneck. Don't choose anything too itchy or hot. Typically, I like a black cotton turtleneck bodysuit for layering. It might sound counterintuitive, but if you have a larger chest, a bodysuit or a more tightly fitted turtleneck is more flattering. Clients with larger chests often assume they should choose something baggy, but that actually makes your chest look bigger, because the shirt will hit your breasts and then just fall. You want something to hug your curves. Even if you're wearing your turtleneck under a blazer or a sweater, go for something more fitted. Just trust me. And, by the way, there's a misconception that you can't wear necklaces outside of your turtleneck—but you can and you should. It brings a little adornment to your style and looks really put together.

1. Wear with truly any bottoms: denim, silk trousers, printed pants, skirts, or shorts.

2. Create polish by wearing your black turtleneck beneath blazers, button-downs, or sweaters, just peeking out at the top.

3. Layer under a dress—picture it beneath a long-sleeved dress paired with high boots to make a chic transition into fall.

4. **ELEGANT. RETRO. MODERN:** Style your turtleneck under a collarless jacket and add jeans to make it feel more casual, but keep the cut straight and fitted to maintain the elegant silhouette. You could even add ballet flats and a pair of cat-eye sunglasses.

5. **CLEAN. CLASSIC. CASUAL:** Style your turtleneck under a boxy white button-down with drapey wide-leg trousers. White sneakers will make a fun call-back to the white button-down.

6. **FUNCTIONAL. LAYERED. SLEEK:** Style a turtleneck under a chunky knit, a warm option with texture and intrigue.

7. **DIANE KEATON** would wear a slim black turtleneck with wide-leg jeans, a hat, and sunglasses. She might even add a funky belt and a button-down or blazer on top.

8. **AUDREY HEPBURN** would wear her black turtleneck with flat-front pants and ballet flats.

9. **NAOMI CAMPBELL** would wear a black turtleneck with a leopard coat and an amazing pair of boots.

4. A Cozy Sweater

A cozy and comfortable sweater transcends the very idea of clothing, becoming something so much more. An amazing sweater that you can throw on with anything is like a security blanket. It's the thing you cuddle up in after a long day at work. It's the comfort you take with you when you travel, whether you wear it on the plane or snuggle up with it in a hotel room far away from home. Everyone needs an emotional support sweater. I personally have a few that I love to wear no matter what. I throw one on over my workout clothes or for Zoom calls. All I ask is that your cozy sweater makes you feel safe, snug, and also dressed. If you are someone who loves crewnecks, go crew. If you want another turtleneck, have at it! Want a V-neck? Sure! I'm not going to put restrictions on color, neckline, fabrication, or fit. Personally, I like cashmere because it is extra soft and easy. If you're buying something new, select a color that works with your wardrobe. Whether it's more of a statement or something simple and neutral, just make sure the color enhances what you already have.

1. Wear your sweater with a pair of smart trousers to add a little softness to a tailored look. You're allowed to tuck in a sweater. I love a tucked sweater, which is how I wear mine with jeans and my fave blazer. For those who want to define the waistline, hiding under a sweater might seem unappealing. But when you do a little front tuck, you look more styled and you draw the eye to the waistline.

2. I like to use a cozy sweater as a belt, tying it around my waist when I'm wearing a dress that needs a little definition at the midline. Or tie it around your neck like a scarf when you are wearing a blazer or trench, adding some soft texture to your look.

3. Style your sweater with a pair of leggings and an overcoat for an easy, off-duty look.

4. **ROMANTIC. BOHEMIAN. LUXE:** Wear a boxy turtleneck sweater with a maxi skirt and leather knee-high boots.

5. **ECLECTIC. PREPPY. JOYFUL:** Try a classic cable-knit sweater with an animal print maxi skirt and ballet flats.

6. **CLASSIC. AMERICANA. TAILORED:** Wear it with a denim shirt underneath—just push the sleeves up and leave the collar peeking out at the top.

7. **CAROLYN BESSETTE-KENNEDY** would wear her cozy sweater with a silk slip skirt and flats. Wear it over your shoulders with a sexy slip dress to soften the style.

8. Go for an **ALEXA CHUNG** look by throwing your cozy sweater over a frilly piecrust-collar blouse and pairing with a miniskirt and mules.

9. **TRACEE ELLIS ROSS** would go for a cozy knit in a bold color and pair it with colorful trousers.

5. The Blazer

If you didn't know, I'm here to tell you—I'm a huge fan. A blazer adds structure to your look, as well as angles and a hint of hardness, no matter your style. It can make any outfit more polished. That's why finding the right blazer for every single person out there is my mission! Some of my clients who spent too many years resentful of the blazers they wore to work or who don't want to look too corporate are hesitant to slip into a blazer. I get it. You can alleviate those worries by trying blazer styles that won't make you feel like you're trapped behind a desk. Try one with a texture or pattern—a houndstooth, check, or pinstripe. You may still want a second, more simple option in a solid color too. However, black can feel a bit too serious. If that's the case, try navy, brown, or camel—something that can be worn with anything but doesn't feel quite as stark. If you go for black—the all-time classic— have a little more fun with the shape. Try something longer or with stronger shoulders, just to make it feel modern.

Don't be afraid to get your blazer professionally tailored. Blazers are a great thing to find secondhand, but they sometimes require alterations. Even if you are petite you can make an oversized blazer work. In order to keep the jacket from overwhelming your smaller frame, have the sleeves tailored so that they hit at or slightly above your wrists. This easy alteration makes all the difference and keeps the jacket from looking sloppy. In the same way, pushing up

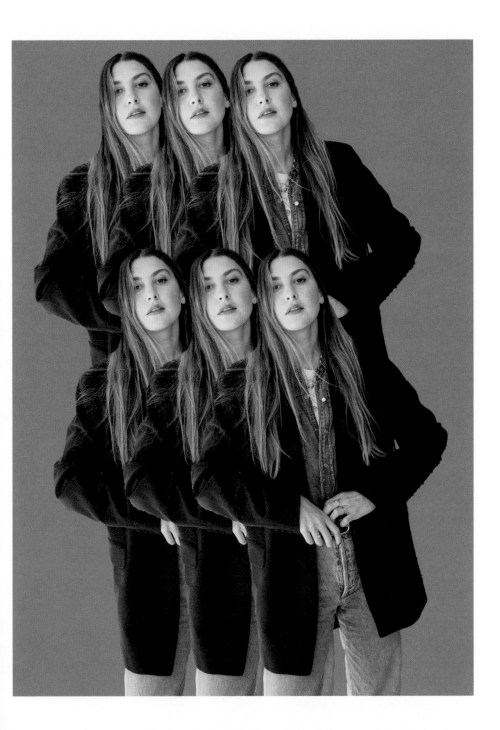

or rolling the sleeves—and showing a little skin—will also create more balance.

1. To accentuate your waist, or if you have a larger chest, wear your blazer open over something fitted, like a bodysuit, drawing the eye to the midline. Even if the blazer is relaxed, this balanced look is flattering and clean.

2. I like to think of the blazer as an indoor coat, something you can wear to work or indoors in the wintertime, even if you wear it underneath a big overcoat or trench coat when you go outside. That way you can feel dressed and styled indoors, but also nice and warm.

3. Don't be too precious with your blazer. Push up the sleeves and mess it up a little just to make it feel like it's yours. Since blazers are more structured, people can feel stiff in them, but it's best to take control of your clothes and wear them in a way that works for you.

4. **CLASSIC. PREPPY. TAILORED:** A checked blazer sandwiched over a turtleneck and under a trench coat, just peeking out from underneath, looks divine. Layering a bunch of classic items together in this way feels anything but basic.

5. **SPORTY. MINIMAL. GRAPHIC:** Style a black blazer with a black cycling short or legging. Add a white tee and some white socks and shoes to give a nice black and white contrast. If you wear leggings, wear socks that are a little longer so you can have them slightly over the leggings for a little texture.

6. **OPULENT. FLOWY. EFFORTLESS:** Throw a blazer over your favorite dress to give a little structure to your flowy look. Add some jewelry, and you have the perfect look for a wedding, an event, or just a fun evening out.

7. **RIHANNA** would wear an oversized leather blazer with a tangle of amazing jewelry and leather pants. She might even wear it bare over a bra to make it super sexy.

8. **BILLY PORTER** would choose a bright-colored blazer and add a fun brooch to spark a playful and vibrant vibe.

9. **JIMI HENDRIX** would choose a velvet blazer, pairing it with printed pants and a silk neck scarf.

6. The Trench Coat

There's nothing as sophisticated and put-together as a trench coat. Sometimes the trench is more present at fashion's forefront, and sometimes it's less relevant. But there has never been a bad time to wear a trench coat. In fact, it creates the perfect balance, sedating any look that seems too trendy, wild, or colorful with a strong shot of minimal chic. If the trench coat feels a little too stuffy or traditional for you, that's part of its appeal. The trench makes a great juxtaposition as a strong, structured anchor. The mandate, however, is to choose a classic. I recommend opting for a trench that doesn't have too many trendy touches. You want to get wear out of this item for years to come. Along those lines, remember: cotton and easy to clean. You don't want a trench that feels too precious or fussy.

If the classic khaki color just isn't working for you, you could try green, navy, or black. As long as the shape is classic, it will give you what you need. If the shape feels too stiff, go for a slightly more flowy or drapey version, but still cut in the classic khaki color. If the whole thing feels too classic altogether, maybe try a leather trench. This option maintains the traditional shape but adds an edge. If you are petite, go for something that hits just above or just below the knee. This creates length without making you feel like you are drowning. I know some petite women think they can't wear a trench, but the magic is in the proportion. That said, a taller person might choose a longer trench that hits right above the ankle. This creates a cool, oversized look, while retaining the trench's classical perfection.

1. Be creative with how you belt and close your trench. There are many ways to tie it. Or swap out the matching belt for a cool belt of your own, just to mix it up. For those who like to show off the waistline, you'll find that the cinch is really flattering.

2. The trench is a great piece for business travel or time spent in the business world. Layer it over a blazer or a suit, bringing together several classic pieces in a way that feels interesting and bringing a little fluidity to balance the tailoring.

3. Great as a layer over a denim jacket.

4. **WHIMSICAL. SIMPLE. SEXY:** Wear your trench open over an amazing floral dress or even shorts. It's a great piece to layer over something sexier, giving your look that traditional vibe.

5. **SEVENTIES. EFFORTLESS. POLISHED:** Style a classic double-breasted trench with a silk tie-neck blouse and flared denim. Wear it open and tie the belt loosely in the back. This will create a nice, easy-breezy look.

6. **TOUGH. STRUCTURAL. DARING:** Try a leather trench or a trench with shoulder pads to create a little structure. You could even tie the belt super tight to exaggerate the proportion and play up the strong shoulders.

7. **ANDRÉ LEON TALLEY** would wear a trench over a three-piece suit styled with gloves and sunglasses. Even though the trench is simple and classic, he would make it feel incredibly intricate and special.

8. **MINDY KALING** would style a trench with a printed, pleated skirt and a matching sweater, giving the traditional trench a quirky and playful look.

9. **JACKIE KENNEDY** would wear hers with a turtleneck and clean, slim pants. And she would add a signature pair of sunglasses and a silk scarf.

The Nine Universal Pieces

7. Denim

Finding your perfect pair of jeans is like dating. You might have to search a little, but it only takes one. A great pair of jeans makes you feel amazing, like the best version of you. I know it can be discouraging to try on a million pairs of jeans that don't work, but prepare yourself for that possibility and commit to staying with it until you find the right one. My advice when it comes to trying denim is more is more—try as many pairs as you can. And no matter what your Three Words are, a pair of jeans that you just love to wear is essential.

1. There are very few occasions, except for the most formal, where denim would be inappropriate. Designers even show jeans with their runway collections these days. But how you style your denim makes all the difference. You can wear the same vintage Levi's with a T-shirt and sneakers for a walk in the park or with chic slingbacks and a silk blouse for a work meeting.

2. Denim amplifies the casualness of any look. When worn with an amazing sequin jacket and heels, denim brings your style back down to earth.

3. In the workplace, you can dress denim up a bit to feel polished. I love pairing it with a blazer for work. I always add a belt to give that finishing touch.

4. **AMERICANA. CLASSIC. PREPPY:** Try denim on denim! Wear your jeans with a soft chambray button-down and a pair of loafers. If denim on denim feels too intense, add a white tee under your denim shirt and unbutton it a little or wear it open. This will break up the look a bit and make it feel less intense. I like when the denim colors are similar, but if it feels too matchy, try a lighter denim shirt with some dark denim jeans.

5. **BOURGEOIS. TAILORED. ACADEMIC:** Go for straight-leg denim with a crisp white button-down and add a black cashmere sweater on top. Tuck in the shirt so only the collar is visible to give a polished look. Top it all off with a houndstooth blazer and a pair of kitten-heeled booties for a prim and proper spin.

6. **TRENDY. GLAM. SPORTY:** Choose high-waisted denim with a high-neck bodysuit and leather bomber. Finish it off with gold hoop earrings and a pair of chunky-soled boots.

7. **SOFIA COPPOLA** would wear high-waisted straight-leg jeans with a striped sweater and a pair of ballet flats.

8. **PENNY LANE** would flaunt flared denim with an embroidered blouse, a shaggy jacket, and platforms.

9. **FRAN LEBOWITZ** would choose vintage Levi's, a white button-down shirt, a blazer, and boots.

Shopping for Denim

How high should the waist be? Should you get a wide leg? When you are choosing your jeans style, go for what suits you. As I'm writing this book, skinny jeans are out. I don't think this means that you can't wear skinny jeans. But maybe this is an opportunity to try something with a slim leg that isn't tight around the ankle. Who knows, you might love flares. I want people to wear what they like and what makes them feel amazing, but I also love it when people can have fun and not be afraid to try something new. When we take baby steps, experimentation is easier. Take it slow. Give yourself a second. If you still love your skinnies, then great—wear them. Everything comes back around.

When shopping for jeans, create a denim dressing room in the comfort of your own home. Bring home a few different sizes and a few different styles and have a denim party. Try on your denim with all kinds of different tops, jackets, and shoes to get a solid sense of what works with what you already own. Remember—returning clothes is just plain annoying, and a place where you can lose steam. Get all the sizes you're interested in at once so you can return everything together instead of spending time going back and forth.

DETERMINE WHERE YOU WANT TO WEAR YOUR JEANS. You should have some that are really comfortable. But, very honestly, the best-fitting denim is slightly uncomfortable—it's just a little tight. While it's not what you want to lounge around in all the time, it looks amazing. You can be discerning about when and where you want to exercise your right to wear something a little more fitted, stiff, and sexy. Not a look for every day.

SIZING IS UNPREDICTABLE. Sometimes you think something fits, but it's really nice to have the next size up and the next size down handy, just to compare and contrast. You don't want to be stuck with jeans that are unintentionally a little too snug or uncomfortably baggy. And for everyday wear, you don't want to feel uncomfortable or look uncomfortable and ruin your day over something small. It's not worth it.

FOR SOME REASON, WE ALL THINK THAT JEANS SHOULD FIT AS SOON AS WE GET THEM. But a lot of denim needs to be hemmed or tailored. As a rule of thumb, if you have a small waist and larger hips, choose a size up and have the waist taken in slightly by a tailor. It will make you feel so good to have jeans that fit.

LOOKING INTO YOUR CLOSET, determine which tops you're wearing most frequently. If you're gravitating to boxy, oversized, or flowy tops, then try denim that is on the slim or straight-legged side, or even something that is fitted in the thigh and flares a little.

IF YOUR FAVORITE TOPS ARE FITTED, CROPPED, OR BODYSUITS, why not try a wide-leg or relaxed-lift denim style to balance things out?

LENGTH IS AN IMPORTANT CONSIDERATION. If you are petite, don't go cropped. The most universally flattering place for jeans to hit is at your ankle bone (the widest part of your ankle). The eye moves to the place where the pants stop. When you end that line above your ankle, your leg will look shorter. We create a nice long line by keeping the eye moving. No matter how tall you are, when you choose high-waisted jeans that are flared to the ground (or at least to your ankle bone), your legs look a mile long.

IF YOU HAVE A SHORT TORSO AND LONG LEGS, try a mid- or even low-rise to balance your silhouette.

8. Trousers

Trousers are chic but also comfortable. As with the trench coat, sometimes trousers are the height of fashion, and sometimes they aren't. But they always bring a shot of grown-up attitude to your style. Even if one of your Three Words is *playful* or *bohemian*, trousers can work for you—especially on those occasions when you need to usher in a little seriousness. After all, the more quiet and sensible your trousers are, the more you amplify the playfulness and the fun of your other pieces. You might not wear trousers every day, but they will deliver a lot to your wardrobe.

You can invest a little in trousers that won't require dry-cleaning after each wear. You can also find great vintage and secondhand trousers. While they usually require alterations, think of this expense as an investment, especially if your trousers are a lucky thrift-store score. To narrow in on the right trousers, I use my denim preferences as a guide. So, if you like your jeans with a slimmer leg, start by looking for slim-cut trousers. Just look through your wardrobe and make sure that the trousers you like will hang easily with what you already own, allowing you to wear your favorite pieces in a whole new way.

1. Trousers are a great item to turn to when you don't know what to wear. Style your trousers with a black turtleneck and amazing accessories for a super-sleek look that you can wear literally anywhere.

2. Wide-leg trousers with a classic front pleat look amazing with a T-shirt and sneakers or with a tank top and chunky sandals.

3. You can style trousers with a button-down or with a silk blouse for work, but they can also be worn with a blazer to create a suited look.

4. **BEACHY. SIMPLE. UNEXPECTED:** Pick linen trousers with a front pleat and a lower rise to create a relaxed and slouchy vibe. Style with a pair of Birkenstocks, a fitted ribbed tank, and some beaded jewelry.

5. **TONAL. ETHEREAL. SLOUCHY:** Try camel trousers with a cashmere sweater in a light brown. Style with a suede flat and a slouchy hobo bag.

6. **EDGY. WITCHY. WESTERN:** Go for high-waisted slim black pants with a sheer silk chiffon blouse and a suede belt. (Think of a Hedi Slimane–era Saint Laurent vibe.)

7. **KATHARINE HEPBURN** would wear high-waisted wide-leg trousers and a button-down for a menswear-inspired look.

8. **PHOEBE PHILO** would wear navy relaxed wide-leg trousers with a gray crewneck sweater, clean white sneakers, and a low ponytail for a minimal and clean look.

9. **BIANCA JAGGER** would choose flared white trousers with a fitted vest and a pair of platforms.

Tuck In

A front tuck, or as Tan France calls it, the *French tuck*, is nice with almost anything. This simply means tucking a bit of the front hem of your T-shirt into the waistband of your pants. The rule of thumb is to only tuck the portion that sits between your first two belt loops if you were tucking into jeans. Without loops, use the center of the waistband on your skirt or trousers. That way it will look a little undone rather than very precise. And don't worry about perfection here. Trust yourself—and what YOU think looks right.

Getting the Fit

Not everyone knows how to work with a tailor, but taking your clothes to an expert to have them fitted just to suit you is a huge style boost! Here are some of my favorite ways to work with the professionals to innovate—and get a great fit.

Bring several pairs of shoes of different heights when you take trousers to the tailor. That way you can have the trousers altered so that you can wear them with either heels or flats. Ultimately, you'll go for something in between. Worn with flats or sandals, trousers should just barely graze the ground. Having a slight break at the bottom, near the ankle, is also nice, creating a more relaxed look. Worn with a higher heel, trousers should be slightly shorter while still completely covering the ankle and, ideally, just hitting the top of the foot.

Change up the buttons on blazers and coats. This is a great way to make vintage or thrifted pieces feel more modern.

If a jacket or blazer feels too big or boxy, have the sleeves tailored to your wrists. This makes the fit look more intentional and less sloppy.

If you love button-downs but feel like they either look too buttoned up or leave you too exposed, showing off your bra when you'd rather not, add a hook and eye between the buttons so that you can create an open, easy look without going too far.

9. Belt

The finishing touch. A belt is like a bow on top of a present. It is that final element that makes almost any look feel more styled, with very minimal effort. A belt elevates the most basic combination, tying it all together so that things feel complete. Many clients are nervous to wear a belt because they feel like it will draw unwanted attention to their waistline, or their "pooch." Not true! But I get it. While it can seem weird to tuck in your top and draw attention to an area that might not be your fave, wearing a belt actually helps create a really flattering silhouette. If you just leave your shirt to hang down over your unbelted jeans, the hemline of the top cuts you off visually and bisects your body. Tucking in and adding a belt establishes a more fluid and intentional line rather than something harsh. It's all about striking a nice balance. The very act of putting the belt on will make you feel styled. It's that one extra piece that takes almost any look to the next level. You'll be surprised how a small thing can make such a big impact.

1. A belt is a great way to add a pop to your look—but it doesn't necessarily need to be colorful to pop. You can use a black belt with an all-white look for interesting contrast, or a brown or tan belt with an all-black look for a neutral balance. Even if you style a black belt with an all-black look, the belt's texture and hardware can add contrast.

2. A belt guides your purposeful front tuck. Simply tuck in your top or sweater just behind the buckle, as if showing it off. This gives you a reason for the tuck in and looks really polished and easy. For example, you can tuck a silk shirt behind the belt to avoid a bumpy look. It also breaks up the lines and shows off your waist.

3. I love the idea of cinching your waist with a belt over a coat, jacket, or dress. If you're wearing an oversized jacket but usually prefer a more fitted silhouette, you can create a waist, or the illusion of a waist, by belting your jacket. Belting can change the silhouette of a piece and create a totally new shape. You can also swap out the belt that comes with a coat or belted dress with a leather belt to wear your piece in a different way.

4. A braided belt is versatile because you can insert the prong anywhere along the length to accommodate your waist or hips.

5. I like a chunky or more menswear-inspired belt paired with something a bit lighter and softer in texture.

6. When you wear a belt that has more prominent hardware, it brings a little polish to your look—like jewelry.

7. **PRINCESS DIANA** would wear a suede belt with a pair of high-waisted jeans and a white button-down. A simple look made from all Universal pieces.

8. **EMMANUELLE ALT** would embolden a pair of slim leather trousers with a belt with a bit of hardware. To balance the edge with a little softness, she would pair with a T-shirt, a blazer, and a small pointed-toe kitten heel.

9. **MICHELLE OBAMA** often belts her blazers or dresses to create a great silhouette.

Accessorize with Love

Accessories are never extra—they are central to expressing your style and offer you the chance to really infuse your personality into every look. While I could probably write a whole book just on accessories, I want to point out a few foundational philosophies that have come to help me use accessories well.

JEWELRY AND BELTS MAKE A HUGE IMPACT. Even the act of adding something to your look says, *I really did something here!*

THINK ABOUT TEXTURE when working with accessories, how hardware or fabrics can bring something new to your look.

SOCKS can bring a great peek of color and surprise to your look.

SCARVES SHOULD BE COMFORTABLE and never too precious. If you are nervous to wear a scarf, choose a low-stakes event to push into your comfort zone.

SUNGLASSES HAVE SO MUCH PERSONALITY. It can be great to keep three pairs of sunglasses around, to reflect each one of your Three Words. That way they bring instant balance to any look.

WEARING JEWELRY GIVES YOU A THROUGH LINE and can help you carry your look from one day to the next with consistency and personality.

I LOVE GOING WITH THE "WRONG" SHOE CHOICE, which is to say the least obvious choice. Shoes make or break a look, and if you always choose what's obvious or basic, then a look can feel, well . . . basic. I often try a shoe that feels a little out of the box. It changes the entire look.

SAME WITH THE BAG. You can use a bag to create balance or tension. If your look is menswear-inspired, try a ladylike top-handle bag to mix it up. If you're wearing a more structured look, maybe choose a slouchy bag. Playing with these unexpected details can be really creative.

part four

Make Dressing a Joyful Ritual

How Do I Create a New Look?

chapter ten

While skeptics might doubt some of the everyday practices I've offered so far, I promise that these simple shifts truly have the power to transform your days. I've seen it happen time and again with my clients, and it can happen for you. So far we've covered clearing out your closet with the AB Closet-Editing System by wrangling your Regulars, Nevers, and Hows; discovering your Three Words; and building out your wardrobe with the Nine Universal Pieces. We'll complete the process in the next chapter by experimenting with how to use Base pieces and Formulas as frameworks to create new looks through a system of slight variations.

Not only will these techniques take the stress out of getting dressed, but—even better—they will also turn the time you spend with your closet into an opportunity to nurture your creativity and care for yourself. You don't need to wear something new every day and reinvent the wheel. You just need to find something that makes you feel confident and strong—and like yourself. And why not experience a little expansion along the way?

The reason I love to plan and catalog and create new looks—beyond the fun of flexing my creativity—is because it helps make life easier. Simplifying, strategizing, and eliminating decision fatigue are great ways to create ease. You'll start with your favorites and build on them, grounding yourself with these go-to pieces, and you'll slowly come out of your comfort zone. But beyond the practical—creating looks can be fun. Be creative and don't judge yourself. Give yourself time to experiment, without expectations or goals. Mess around with something new and, if it doesn't work—it's okay. It's all information that you can use. Try on your craziest things just to see. And remember: no stress. If you find yourself reaching for the same thing every time, that's also okay. Consistency and an understanding of what you know is never bad. It's powerful. And if you still want to challenge yourself, wear what you normally grab, but change one thing. You don't have to totally reinvent yourself. There are small changes that will make you feel excited and confident enough to go even further. Here, I'll share some ways to build a supportive structure to keep you far above the fray.

Covering Your Bases & Finding Your Formulas

A *Base* is the first layer of clothing that you put on before you style it up—the bones of the look. It might be jeans and a tee. Or a dress, or a sweater with trousers. I described my favorite Bases earlier in the Nine Universal Pieces section (page 118), but you may have other pieces that you love to build on, especially among your Regulars. Once you've identified your Bases, you can clearly see how many variations are possible when you build off of each one. We're going to take your Bases and create some go-to combos—your *Formulas*.

It's easy to grasp this concept if you think about style icons like Diane Keaton or Stevie Nicks. Each is known for a clearly defined look. Diane Keaton's signature Formula consistently includes several—wide-legged pants, a tight turtleneck, and an over-shirt or blazer, with a fun accessory, like a hat or scarf. Stevie Nicks uses a belt to add a little structure and shape to her favorite flowy dresses. Finding your Formulas is about sticking to what you love and staying true to it at the foundation of the look. You can have fun bringing your expressive flair to these Formulas day by day.

Let's look at how one of my clients, Gabrielle, found her Bases and Formulas to build new looks. Gabrielle lives in Washington, DC, has a government job, and travels constantly. She's a lifelong learner and took our sessions very seriously—she always wants to understand *why*.

Gabrielle certainly doesn't have a lot of time to worry about what to wear, especially in the morning, and you probably don't either. Before we collaborated, she had a huge wardrobe full of a ton of things, most of which she never wore. Through the closet-editing process, we homed in on what she loved and what got her excited. We worked with her Three Words—*functional*, *exaggerated*, and *tailored*—and we rounded out her wardrobe with new essentials (crisp button-downs and jewelry to layer with her more delicate pieces). And then came the part she learned to love most—building new looks.

In order to identify Gabrielle's Bases, I had her slip on her go-to work clothes, which were most often button-down shirts and slim pairs of Rag & Bone trousers. This was her first Base—the bones of her look before we added a jacket or styled it up using jewelry and accessories. Once you have your Base you can create a Formula by adding to it and creating different variations. For example, her Base was a button-down and trousers, and one of the Formulas we created was button-down + trousers + blazer+ loafers.

Next, we switched out her button-down for a favorite silky blouse, to create a second Base, and we followed the same process, taking pictures with different combinations. We eventually explored all of her favorite pieces for work outfits, changing them one at a time. As you can imagine, we wound up with an insanely rich album of different variations on her tried-and-true look and made many new discoveries along the way. Then we started again with her weekend looks, beginning with her favorite jeans and a striped nautical T-shirt that was in high rotation, and creating variations on that Formula with jackets, blazers, and button-downs.

Gabrielle's Formulas were: button-down + slim trousers, blouse + slim trousers, sweater + slim trousers, sweater + wide-leg trousers, blouse + jeans, button-down + jeans. And her Formulas were plentiful as we tried each of these with different jackets, shoes, and accessory combos. Some looks suited her Three-Word combination more than others. Gabrielle could use the portfolio of pictures we'd taken to decide what to wear when planning her week or when packing for a work trip. She felt relieved and liberated, like she had the headspace to think about other things.

We created some foolproof new Formulas for when Gabrielle began traveling for work again, including looks for the airplane. Now when she gets a new travel assignment, she can focus on her work because she knows exactly what she will pack and what she

will wear. And if she runs into a client in the airport, she knows that she will look and feel great. That kind of reassurance is so valuable—it's true peace of mind and a beautiful expression of self-care.

When Gabrielle started to plan out her looks and invest a little time in her expression, she began to field a lot of compliments. Even if she was wearing a simple button-down and trousers, the care she put into her look was obvious. Her own sense of strength and confidence shone through, and her coworkers and friends responded to that energy shift. Their glowing feedback made her feel even more inspired to try new combinations and be even more creative. When we first started working together she was skeptical about pairing a bright white button-down with cream-colored trousers because she thought "the colors were off," but she now mixes and matches her neutrals like a pro! Her weekend looks are equally considered.

You can follow the process Gabrielle and I went through. Once you have defined your Bases and built your Formulas, you can change it up. For example, if you know your favorite combo is T-shirt + blazer + jeans, then you can play with the different ways to approach this Formula, like wearing a graphic or colorful T-shirt or trying different styles of jeans.

Let's be honest. Sometimes we really just don't have the time. I repeat variations of the same look all the time. To me, outfit repeating is actually a sign of someone who is confident and knows their style. After all, if you're always changing up your aesthetic, that means that you haven't yet connected with who you really are! Once I find a Formula that works, I'll repeat it and create different variations. For example, in summer I love to wear silk pants and a tank top. I switch up the tank or add a chunky sandal to lend the look a little toughness. I can also go for a kitten heel and blazer to dress it up. And they just keep growing—make a commitment that whenever you buy something new, you'll take just a few minutes to style it and snap photos, weaving it into your favorite Formulas and looks.

The Lookbook

Photograph your looks as you go. I often tell clients to crop out their heads, just so they don't get too picky or judgmental. Still, occasionally I'll include my head in the frame because it reminds me how great I was feeling at that moment (good enough to take a photo of my look!). Photos are valuable not only to plan ahead but also to figure out what isn't working. Maybe you have a top that doesn't quite jibe with anything. You'll know it's time to edit it out and give it up for donation when you see the cold, hard evidence in your photo folder. I might think an item in my wardrobe is great for me, but if I never end up wearing it outside the house, I know there's an issue.

Tried and True

Here are some quick solutions for when you feel like you have nothing to wear.

Flip it. Your first resource should be your Lookbook. Choose one you've never tried before.

On repeat. Put on what you wore the day before but switch up *one* thing. If you wore jeans and a T-shirt, try the same Base combination but add an accessory. Or try black jeans instead. Or swap in a tank for a T-shirt.

Get inspired. Choose a look from your mood board (see The Joy of Pictures, page 100) and try to re-create it using only what you have. I do this often and love creating the same vibe or a similar Formula as a look in my mood board. Whatever I come up with is usually a very loose interpretation, but it's fun and creative and really gives me momentum when I'm stuck. A note on copying: Creating new looks becomes super un-fun when we aren't true to ourselves, when we try to copy and paste something we saw someone else wear, or when we try to co-opt someone else's aesthetic without funneling it through our own Three Words. This is exactly what leads to feelings of inadequacy and brings out the voices that tell us we don't have the "right" clothes. You can always find a way to make a look that you love your own! Don't give up and give in.

Footloose. You can really cultivate personal style with your footwear. You'll be amazed. Choose an outfit that you love to wear, but change the shoe for something completely different. It's an easy way to make a big transformation, especially when you are feeling daring enough to try shoes that you imagine "don't go" or wild cards that take your look to the next level.

Deeper Analysis

I love looking back through my photos to workshop why a look isn't happening. The why is important. I have a few clients who take photos of what they wear every single day—even if they don't love the look—and this gives us a whole lot of data to work with. One client, who was having a hard time choosing clothes she felt had the right proportions for her body, sorted all of her images into two folders—"successful" and "less successful." Within the "successful" folder, she grouped together all the looks whose proportions she liked. Then she made a list of attributes that the successful looks had in common. Through this process, we learned that she clearly loved high-necked and low-backed tops, and she felt good when her pants were cut higher-waisted. It was all distilled so beautifully. We were also able to peek at her less flattering images to figure out what she should avoid in the future and how she could tweak and restyle those looks to suit her proportions.

Weekly Practice

I love to set aside at least twenty minutes each week to plan and try on looks for the week ahead. And, truly, this is just as crucial—or more so—as anything else we've done so far. You can guess how many times I've heard the excuse that you don't have time. But this is the prep work that actually saves you time throughout the week, a gift you can give to yourself. And I bet if you give it a try, this weekly ritual will turn into a creative, adventurous time that you actually look forward to and appreciate. I know it might sound crazy to think about what you'll wear for the week, including an outfit for the farmers market on Sunday, but the benefit is in waking up and knowing you have pampered yourself by setting aside a look that makes you feel amazing. It's about taking pride in everything you do.

I usually schedule this time for Sunday at the end of the day, when I have my makeup on, because it always makes what I'm wearing feel that much better. If I don't feel cute, I won't really like anything I try on—so this is good support for me. To get the most out of your time, make it really indulgent. Create a mood, light a candle, pull up your mood board, and put on some music or a TV show. This is a great time to look at the images that inspire you for a little guidance.

Fly Free

Your weekly session is a good time to go freestyle. Beyond the looks you've documented and banked in your phone, try on things that you haven't before. Or put on something you always wear, but with new accessories. This is a safe space to experiment and analyze, which will bolster your confidence. You are building towards feeling really good in what you're wearing—every day!—which doesn't happen when you are late and running out the door. When Gabrielle got into the swing of pulling her looks together once a week, she had a creative burst. She broke apart a gray herringbone suit and paired the pants with a new cream double-breasted blazer and black turtleneck. Then she tried on a black blazer instead. I think she loved the way she looked, for sure, but she also loved feeling in command of her style, and that she was growing into and expressing her true self in ever-expanding ways.

Everyday Rituals: Your Daily Routine Reenvisioned

Now, thanks to your devotion to this process, you have a vast array of looks to choose from right there at your fingertips, and the practical part is done. Your daily practice is to sink into the delicious beauty of the moment as you get yourself ready for your day. How good will that feel? So many of us dread figuring out what to wear in the morning, whether we're bored by the options or feel uncomfortable or "less than" when we get dressed. But already, by simply reframing the way you think about getting dressed, you can start to shift the heaviness and create some gentle structure, transforming this time from something depleting and draining into a ritual that supports your self-expression. You start by asking yourself, *How do I want to feel today?* The way you feel in what you wear is foundational, the most important requirement informing whatever you choose to wear. You may have planned something to wear, but how does that choice sit with you in the moment?

Getting Dressed

I recommend setting aside twenty minutes to get dressed in the morning. Never rush; let everything flow smoothly. I promise, a peaceful morning makes all the difference in how you feel for the rest of the day. I like to pull on a robe post-shower and lay out what I'm planning to wear on the bed. It's an easy and maybe unnecessary step, but it sets the tone for my day. We all have busy lives, and the potential for having a chaotic morning is high. The more you can slow down, the better the chances of having a great day. How can you see this time as something you *get* to do, rather than something you *have* to do?

I've had clients who shifted their mornings through their approach to dressing and experienced a flow-on effect right away.

They began to eat healthier and take better care of their bodies and their homes. It can inspire so much positive change.

Altars, Inspiration, and Practice

As you prepare for your week ahead or move through your morning, getting ready for whatever lies ahead, there are some small things you can do to anchor your vision and connect in a deeper way with yourself. Your dressing area is a creative space. You can create a little altar to help you focus your intention, a visual representation of your Three Words to hold your inspiration and remind you of who you are, what you like, and what you want to share with the world. I've seen beautiful mandalas collaged together from inspirational images. Maybe a single Polaroid sums it all up for you. It can feel great to juxtapose a 2D image or collage with something beautiful like a candle or flowers. Infuse the whole of it with your imagination. It's my hope that this sense of reverence for yourself and your time seeps into your spirit and becomes part of you. And you can refresh what's surrounding you as often as you like. Switch up your images when things are feeling stale.

You can add to your inspiration, printing out screenshots and cutting out images from magazines and layering them on top of one another, like a constantly evolving vision board. Remind yourself of what's important to you, how you want to feel, and how

you want to move through the world. What would make you feel seen and held and keep you on track?

Like working with a mantra in a yoga class, the altar space grounds you and gets you into what you're doing. When you keep some of your inspiration in the physical realm, you don't have to look at your phone. I had a stool in my closet with a candle and some photos I had printed out—some very clear, inspiring visuals to keep me focused. The candle reminds me that this is a very privileged, indulgent moment that I am lucky to have.

Setting Sets the Tone

Do whatever you have to do to get yourself in the best headspace. I like to have my morning beverage and put on a little music that relaxes me. Instead of trying to pump myself up and orient myself towards the outside world, I look within, soaking in all the peacefulness I can before a busy day. This gives me the space to focus on how I'd love to feel and how my clothes can support that desire. I check in with my inspirational photos for a little guidance, and I check out my Lookbook (see page 172) to consider my options.

All-Day Adaptations

When I choose a look for a day that encompasses a whole lot of different demands, I always think about the end of the day first and work backward from there. If I have a dinner planned after work, I imagine what I'd feel comfortable wearing there and reverse engineer a look for the rest of my day, usually by layering or adding a jacket (for me it's almost always a blazer). While there used to be a lot of hype around the idea of switching up your accessories to transition from day to night or desk to dinner, nobody actually wants to do that. Some of my favorite Formulas work in a multitude of settings, including wearing a blazer + T-shirt + belted jeans + elegant flats. This combination is great for work settings and for dinner, and if I need to elevate it, I can add a scarf or jewelry to take it to the next level—but I wear it the whole day. No need to tote around accessories all day. Similarly, a sweater + T-shirt + trousers + boots is great for a work meeting, and I can always take off the sweater and tie it around my neck.

Swaps

When I get dressed, I don't get it right every time, even working from my Lookbook. Sometimes I have to try different jackets and bags—and especially shoes. I will often try two or three pairs before leaving the house, because a shoe can totally transform a look. I've also learned that sometimes the shoe you would never expect works the best. So it's worthwhile to try a few. In the same way, I often change out my bag. It makes a big difference. While moving your things between bags frequently can seem daunting, I keep my wallet, keys, and lipstick in a small leather pouch, which I simply transfer from bag to bag. That way I always have what I need and can switch out my bag easily and quickly. Highly recommended.

Exit Plan

When I try on clothes in the morning I put everything away as I go, so I don't come home to a crazy mess after working all day. I also leave myself a little time between getting dressed and leaving the house, which gives me the chance to notice if something doesn't feel or look quite right while I still have time to correct it. Remember, feeling confident and comfortable shapes your mindset. All these steps might feel a little picky, but they quickly become habitual—and bring you so much.

Peaceful Pause

Before you leave your dressing area to officially start your day, give yourself one last long and loving look in the mirror. If you work with affirmations, or if you have a mantra that supports your well-being, now is the time for them. If you have a wish for yourself, for your day and what it will hold, give that gift to yourself. Just one slow inhale and exhale can bring a sense of completion and readiness, setting your day off spinning in the right direction.

Once I'm dressed and have completed my morning routine, I feel thoroughly ready for the day. I'm centered and conscious of the way that my clothes make me feel—which is most important—but also what my look is saying to the world. I create an opportunity to channel my unique energy and confidence.

part five

The Flow-On Effect of Fabulous Style

Dressing with Ease

As we reach the end of our process, we're ready to take all your amazing momentum and spin it around, allowing the way you dress to create a ripple effect. On the deepest level, discovering your style is another way of knowing yourself, and through that clear understanding of what you like and why, fashion can become an outward manifestation of your inner self. Over time, you become fluent in translating who you are into what you wear, and that fluency extends to other areas of your life—how you communicate, the decisions you make, and what you envision for yourself. It has the potential to touch every area of your life—your career, relationships, and sense of happiness. When we feel empowered to say no to what doesn't suit or serve us and yes to what we love, our confidence builds daily.

Sometimes all this requires is merely a simple mindset shift. Remember my client Angela from Chapter Six, who merged her love of romantic and sporty clothes into a seamless style all her own. It was fascinating to see the flow-on effect this had all around her, creating a sense of coherence in her environment and bringing excitement to her daily life. By working out her Three Words, she was able to reconcile competing aesthetics in her apartment. Her home office, where she didn't like to spend time, was more austere and modern, while the rest of her home was layered and textured with bohemian warmth. We realized she had a tendency to want to keep "like with like," the bohemian things with the bohemian things and the austere with the austere. But her true style developed as she embraced her instinctual dynamic and began to mix it up. She added warmer elements to her home office and cultivated the cozy-meets-sleek look in the rest of her space. She started feeling good spending time there, and it showed in her work.

Our collaboration together also gave her a different perspective on her beauty look. She has gorgeous, naturally wavy, thick, dark hair, which she usually wears down, undone, and a little wild. At the same time, her skin care regimen is epic—she loves taking good care of her skin and splurging on makeup. When we met, she was troubled by the idea that these two aspects of herself contradicted each other. But by working with her wardrobe, Angela received a valuable reframe—she could understand her opposing approaches to hair and makeup as creating balance. She gave herself permission to indulge in a nighttime hydration mask and to skip the hair rollers. And that simple, fresh outlook let her experiment more too—if she decides to start pulling her hair into a 'do, she might wear a nude lip to strike a balance that feels more authentic.

The On-Off Switch

Another way that I've seen these wardrobe practices create astounding effects for my clients is through the subtle psychological transformations they spark. For example, you can use your wardrobe to reset your work-life balance by using a simple after-work outfit change to signal to your psyche that it's time to relax.

Many of us work in environments that require us to dress with more polish than we choose to embrace in our daily lives. I will always think of my dad who, every day when he came home from work as I grew up, would say, "One minute—let me just change into my play clothes." For my dad, slipping out of his button-down and khakis and into a T-shirt and jeans signaled the end of the day. While your work clothes should still feel like you, you want your time at home to allow a deeper level of comfort.

Work It Out

So many of my clients have welcomed the evolution of the office into a more casual place, and yet it has left a lot of women in an awkward position, forced to walk a fine line between looking approachable and looking professional. We all want to be taken seriously, but we don't want to look uptight—especially when our coworkers and supervisors are wearing jeans and hoodies to work.

My clients in the tech space want to look "cool," but not sloppy. And we all want to command respect without appearing too overdressed. We want to express our style but not be recognized solely for our look. It can be exhausting.

This is where your Three Words can be super helpful. As you build your holistic wardrobe, the idea is to be consistent, to feel like yourself no matter where you are—at work, at a casual dinner with friends, or at a special event. Instead of having a separate work wardrobe and life wardrobe, your Three Words will help you put together a style that makes you feel good in your own skin. And when you feel good, you get more done and do better work!

WFH

I'm still a head-to-toe girl, no exceptions. Because fashion is wellness, wearing a crisp button-down paired with ratty sweatpants for your video call misses the point. You want to feel elevated on the inside—it's not about faking it.

So, I'd like to make a case for getting dressed and putting on shoes, even when you are working from home and staying relaxed. For example, I do my work calls in a slide sandal because I need to feel grounded, not like I'm just hanging out on the couch. Getting fully dressed lets your whole self know that it's time to focus. Even if your desk is in your bedroom, you need to wear something different than what you slept in. We take our cues from

our environment. Creating this energetic shift in the day is healthy, whether your morning commute is miles long or mere feet.

Still, just as I do when consulting with clients who work in an office environment, my WFH clients each make a Lookbook of variations. If you are in joggers, pair them with a nice cashmere sweater, cute white socks, and a white sneaker. Or pair them with a white T-shirt or a black turtleneck and a flat. The small touches are very impactful.

I love working from home in a cute button-down, jewelry, and favorite leggings. It's worth it to find leggings that are a bit more elevated—not the leggings you'd wear for a workout. They don't have to be expensive, but they shouldn't be athletic gear. And a black turtleneck under a sweatshirt can be such a cool WFH look.

If you're new to working from home, as so many of my clients are, it can feel clarifying to go through your wardrobe with a fresh perspective on your old work clothes and clear out what you aren't wearing anymore. Is it time to cull that black shift dress you used to wear to the office? Do you even like it? Would you wear it on the weekend? The answer is usually no—and some clients even come to realize that black shift dress is actually triggering! Once upon a time, women felt they had to buy these office-y clothes—and they weren't wrong. But the culture has shifted. The narrow suit, that shift dress, and those pencil pants are probably not what you'd want to wear for a job interview now. (Instead, perhaps it would be a silk blouse with a blazer and trousers.) This is a different time, and if you don't love the work clothes that used to be your go-to pieces, it's okay to move on.

Some of your old work pieces can be restyled—pair your favorite work trousers with a T-shirt and sneakers, or, for a Zoom call, with a blazer. Many clients have silk blouses that they used to wear to the office. Instead of wearing these with trousers, try them with high-waisted jeans and boots.

Anytime/Anywhere Dressing

It can feel really good to have a few go-to looks you rely on for in-between times, like picking up the kids, dashing out to the store, or making your way home from the gym. No matter where you are, you're still you. So creating some easy Formulas that help you feel great and grounded while on the go is good support, saving you time and serving your expression.

Here are three of my favorite anytime/anywhere looks.

1. Cashmere sweater + leggings + trench + loafers or sneakers. You can also do the same look with jeans or cycling shorts. The trench makes it feel really sophisticated.

2. Button-down shirt + leggings + loafers. The button-down shirt adds some structure and polish to a classic legging look.

3. Cozy sweater + jeans + belt. The belt is key—I promise if you throw on a cozy knit with your favorite jeans you will feel fabulous, and you will feel even MORE fabulous if you add a belt. The soft sweater and structure create a juxtaposition that feels totally pulled together. If it's super-cold, add a turtleneck underneath, or, if it's just chilly, a white T-shirt.

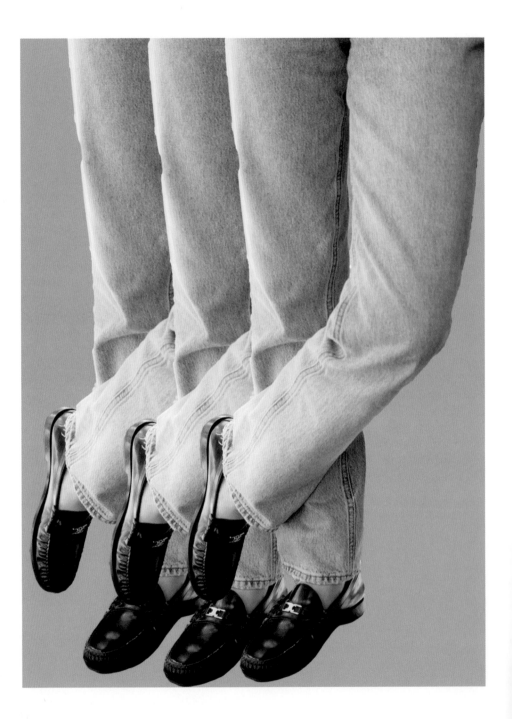

Lounge Love

When it's time to just hang out and watch TV or sit down with your family, I'm big on nice pajamas—whether they are from J. Crew or designer made, you can still feel good in them. But feeling nice when you're lounging at home doesn't mean the T-shirt with the stain, the sweatpants with a hole, or the bodysuit that you cut into a tank. You deserve better than that. Having three nice sets of pj's gives you plenty of options—cozy cotton and silk for warmer months, and for the winter, ribbed or knit pants that you can wear with a vintage T-shirt designated only for lounging.

Fabulous Flats

Comfort is one of the key goals in each of my styling sessions, and the women I meet who once suffered for "beauty" are now donating their high heels and looking for alternatives—a shoe that looks polished but doesn't pinch the toes or leave the arches sore at the end of the day.

My message to you is that an elevated, aesthetically pleasing flat shoe can become part of your look, not just because it's functional and necessary, but as an important part of the fashion. When I was styling an incredible female director, the first thing we talked about was comfort. She was nervous about heading out on a press tour for her first film, so we quickly decided that everything she wore had to make her feel confident. That meant that she couldn't fret about rogue bra straps or fussy silhouettes, and, most importantly, she couldn't stress over uncomfortable shoes. Although a fabulous heel can make you feel powerful, there's subtle strength in wearing a shoe that's so comfortable it means you can stand grounded and serene. The last thing she wanted was to be agonizing over a blister while giving an interview about her incredible new project.

Falling for Flats

CHECK IN WITH YOUR WARDROBE, YOUR MOOD BOARD, AND YOUR THREE WORDS TO ASSESS WHICH KIND OF FLAT COULD WORK BEST FOR YOU. Usually it's something simple and classic. (Personally, I'm a loafer lover.)

BALLET FLATS HAVE A FRENCH-GIRL SEXY APPEAL THAT IS FUN TO TAP INTO. There's so much you can do with a ballet flat, like pairing it with high-waisted Levi's or a pair of cut-off denim shorts. Even if you don't normally go for something that is so demurely feminine—and perhaps especially if you don't!— ballet flats bring a delicate, timeless element to your style.

IF IT ISN'T COMFORTABLE IN THE STORE, IT WON'T BE COMFORTABLE IN REAL LIFE. Sure, some shoes take a few wears to break in, but don't rely on breaking in shoes for your comfort. You have no idea how many of my clients have given away flats because they were uncomfortable from day one.

ADD SOME PERSONALITY TO YOUR STYLING WITH COLORFUL OR TEXTURED SOCKS. Even if they just peek out when you're seated, fun socks are one of those little styling secrets that make you feel pulled together and perfectly you, whether or not anyone else notices.

YOU HAVE AN OPPORTUNITY TO FURTHER EMBRACE WHO YOU ARE WHEN YOU WEAR A FLAT SHOE. If you're petite and have always worn high heels to appear taller, you can explore what it would feel like to shed the notion that you need to be any taller than you are. There's power in that.

GLIDE INTO EFFORTLESSNESS. Flat shoes bring a very different feeling to whatever you're wearing, including looks that you might have styled with a heel in the past. Flats usher in a sense of ease that feels empowering and potent.

Shopping
for Wellness

chapter fourteen

In many ways, this whole process we've embarked on together is about creating a more sustainable wardrobe. The most ecological choice is always going to be what I call Shopping Your Closet, creating new looks using the pieces that you already own.

However, as you become more comfortable with your personal style, as you know who you are and what you like, you become clearer about what you need—and what you don't—and your shopping decisions also make a whole lot more sense. You buy what's necessary. And whether the piece is a major investment or something from Zara, the idea is that whatever your bring into your space you love and really want to wear. No more confusion. No more coming home with things that don't make sense for you and hang in the closet with their tags on.

Wish List

The best way to get the most out of the time you spend shopping is to eliminate decision fatigue. When we have to make too many decisions, we can feel paralyzed. That's why you might keep coming home from your shopping expeditions with the same shirt over and over again. Your brain is overloaded. The best way to eliminate decision fatigue is to keep a wish list. When you see something that you like, add it to your wish list or take a screenshot. Then ask yourself the questions below, which will really help you decide whether to purchase it or not. And by asking yourself these questions ahead of time, when you actually start shopping—whether in person or online—your list will be nice and lean, including only the things that you are actually considering.

These are questions you should ask yourself before committing to any purchase.

1. Do I get a deep-down, full-body *yes* when I see myself wearing this item?

2. Will it make getting dressed easier?

3. Do I have something that serves the same purpose? And if so, when would I wear this new item instead of the piece I already own?

4. Would I be willing to give up something that I have in my wardrobe to own this piece?

5. Will I have to purchase something else in order to wear it? (For example, does it require a specific shoe that I don't own and will have to purchase in addition to the item?)

6. Does it suit my style, or do I really just like the way it looks on someone else? Does it fit with my Three Words?

7. Can I see myself wearing this next year?

8. Will I regret not buying it? (This is what my mom calls "non-buyer's remorse," which can really help you know whether it's time to buy.)

Sale Fever

I love a sale! But the biggest shopping mistakes happen when you buy something on sale just because it is on sale. I see this all the time, and I've made enough mistakes to know the feeling that you failed because you bought something that you can't make work or you simply don't like once it's home. I've learned the hard way that just because something is a good deal doesn't mean it belongs in my wardrobe. This is why I keep a wish list and work in reverse, watching for that magical moment when the items I'm already interested in go on sale, as opposed to shopping the sales without any clue about what I want. It's also important to remember that if you didn't want something when it was full price, you probably don't want it discounted. Think of a sale as a bonus. When the item you already know that you want is on sale, it's that much sweeter.

Save or Splurge?

Here are some tips and strategies for spending intentionally.

When you know you love something but you don't love the price, it can be good to ask yourself, *Would I buy this item even if it wasn't in fashion right now?* There are times when even the most classic pieces wax and wane with the trends. If you would wear something even when it isn't part of the larger style conversation, then it's worth investing in because you'll wear it next season and next year once the trends have moved on.

Items that really maximize your look are worth a little more, like a great handbag or a beautiful coat. These pieces give you a ton of bang for your buck. You'll look pulled together with a great bag, even if you pair it with a T-shirt and leggings. Before committing to a splurge, I like to ask myself, *Is quality part of the value?* For a white T-shirt, it's not—it's cotton, it's easy. It doesn't need to be luxe to have value. But for a nice bag, quality is part of its value, part of what makes it special and part of what you are paying for.

I often see in my work with clients that it can be scary when you arrive at the time in your life when you might want to buy nicer things. Maybe you just started your first big job and are finally earning a great salary, or you got a significant raise. Especially if you've bought fast fashion for a long time, unlocking the idea that you can feel proud of what you choose and can invest in your look can be really empowering. And just because you have the money doesn't mean you have to spend it. Go slowly. You can still use good decision making and commit to choosing things you really love even though your budget is growing.

Another spending strategy I recommend is to invest in tailoring. You can buy jeans almost anywhere these days—the era of $300 denim is over. It is, however, worth spending a little more on tailoring so that your jeans fit perfectly, even if you buy them from the Gap.

Most importantly, however, is this: If your spending is stressful to you, then your wardrobe is not contributing to your wellness, and we need to backtrack a little. Your peace of mind is the most important aspect of this process. Enjoying getting dressed, and using fashion as a way to express yourself and understand who you are in a deeper way, is a process that can bloom over a lifetime. Feeling bad and spending a bunch of money on things you can't afford is moving in the wrong direction.

No Rushing

When you plan your shopping day, only commit to as much as you can take without overdoing it. If your patience is low when shopping and trying things on, be honest and account for that. If you're tired or annoyed or just want to buy something and be done, you will make bad decisions.

There've been times where I felt that if I spent a long time in a store, I had to get something. You absolutely do not. Sometimes when you're shopping you find yourself in a walking trance. Once you leave the shop, you snap out of it—you realize that either you

Trendy vs. Timeless

Here are three questions you can consider when you aren't sure if a purchase is going to be timeless or just a fleeting trend. You want to be clear about discerning whether the things you buy are investment pieces that you plan to wear for a long time, or whether you are jumping into a trend.

Ask yourself:

1. Did I want to wear this last year?

2. Will I want to wear it next year?

3. If this piece comes back in style in ten years, will I want to take out this exact piece and wear it again, or will I want to get a new or updated version? We are essentially minting our own vintage! I love the idea that we can hold on to specific things we will actually wear again.

A timeless piece doesn't have to be an investment—Converse sneakers can be timeless. But in ten years, if you think you'll want to wear Converse again, do you imagine you'll choose the same ones you would wear today? "Timeless" also doesn't have to mean "classic"—a super shaggy shearling coat is timeless, but not necessarily classic. Not everything in your wardrobe needs to be timeless. That would be boring and also might not allow you to express your personality. These questions are personal! It's up to you to define what "timeless" is for you.

actually didn't love any of it, or, hey—actually, you loved that top! This is a shopping tactic I picked up from my grandma. When I was little, we loved shopping together at the mall. We would always choose what we loved, but then put everything on hold before buying and go get lunch or a Frappuccino. Afterwards, we'd come back to try things on and see if we felt sure about a purchase. Giving yourself that space and time feels so good.

In therapy you learn that giving space and time to your decisions is important. Honestly, the simple practice of saying, "Let me think about it and I'll let you know," has changed my life. Take as long as you need. Use shopping as a place where you can build that habit in support of your overall growth.

Good Company

My husband and I both know that shopping together can't work. I like to touch everything and do a couple laps around the store just to make sure I have my bearings, while his patience is limited, and he either follows me (too closely) or waits outside, which makes me feel rushed. The same goes for shopping with kids—or anyone else who makes me feel hurried. That said, I do like shopping with friends who I trust and those who will let me take my time. No matter who you're with, you have to make a commitment to yourself first—do not let anyone talk you into buying things you don't like or need. I have one friend who is fun and encouraging, and always gently brings me out of my comfort zone—but when I'm shopping with her I know

I also need to check my gut. If you love to shop with a particular friend but they aren't available, you can send them a dressing room photo of the finds you love. But here, too, remember to check in with yourself. If you are sending a photo because you aren't sure, that means you probably don't love it. Every time I feel I need to ask, it's because I'm not a full *yes*. The above also holds true for salespeople. Most salespeople are doing their jobs well, and will not try to sell you something that looks awful, but they also don't know what you already have at home, and they do not know you the way you do. Go slow, take your time, and be you.

Dress for It

You should feel comfortable when you're shopping. I like to make sure I'm wearing a good bra when I'm trying on purchases at home or when I head out to shop. My advice is to find a bra that fits well and that you can wear with most things. Foundations are an important part of the look and also hugely affect how you feel. It is worth investing a little in your underwear and bra. It's one of those things that only you know about, but it feels so good to have undergarments that you like wearing.

I usually like to wear my fave jeans and T-shirt when I'm shopping, because whatever I'm buying should usually work with either my favorite jeans or my favorite T-shirt. And, basically, when you wear something you like and that you are comfortable wearing, not only does it remove some of the guesswork, it sets a benchmark. If anything I try is not as cute as what I'm wearing, I don't need it. This is a way of setting yourself up for success.

IRL vs. Online

There is so much joy in browsing in a real store and touching, trying, and seeing things in person. It can also be easier to tell if you actually like something—I've learned that sometimes I'm not interested in things I coveted online when I see them in person. On the downside, once we've dragged ourselves to the store, we can feel pressured to buy so we have something to show for our efforts.

One of the benefits of shopping online is seeing how something is styled. My suggestion is to take the inspiration but leave the limitations behind, using your Three Words and your imagination to overcome any limiting notions. For example, if you see a blouse shown with a pair of ripped jeans and clogs, and you aren't into the bohemian look, you might not envision how it could work for you. If you love the blouse, imagine how you would style it to make it fit with your Three Words.

When I shop in real life, I prefer to wander, but when I shop online, I'm more focused because there is so much out there, so many new things, and so many retailers. We can start to feel that we *need* the newness. That's one of the reasons I opt out of marketing emails except for those from a small group of my very favorite brands—it's hard not to be tempted.

Instant Gratification

One of the things I love about shopping, and I've been like this since I was a kid, is wearing whatever I've bought immediately! When I was little and shopping with my grandma, I'd ask the salespeople to cut the tags so that I could change right then and there, dropping the clothes I'd arrived in into the shopping bag. When I buy something, I want to wear it. This is why I don't recommend buying clothes out of season. If you buy a summer dress in wintertime and it sits in your closet for months, by the time you wear it you might be tired of looking at it and risk never wearing it. If you buy something out of season and you're like me, tuck it away out of sight and give yourself a calendar reminder to take it back out again.

Shopping with Your Style Guide

When I shop, I often channel my two favorite style guides to come along—Jane Birkin and Bianca Jagger. These two fabulous style icons have guided me towards some of my favorite items. This technique can be useful when you need to make a gut check on a potential purchase. Whenever I'm unsure about an item, I ask myself, *Would Jane Birkin buy it?* I also like to channel Harry Styles mixed with Larry David, a little fun and a little boring!

My client Angela found her style guide in French *Vogue* editor Emmanuelle Alt, who could pair a ruffled blouse with leather pants and sneakers in a way that evoked the romantic-sporty vibe Angela was after. When you channel any really powerful style icon, your sense of direction and possibilities becomes very clear. In the same way that you can use your Three Words for support, it's useful to call in an iconic force to help you pause, envision, and be very intentional.

Showing Up as Yourself

chapter fifteen

No matter how you slice it, style is about expressing *you* as only you can do. Every morning you have an opportunity to do just that, allowing the practice of getting dressed to transform you. Recently, I was working with a client and asked them what they liked about the clothes in their closet. They said they liked that the clothes all fit well, but that they wouldn't care if they opened their closet door tomorrow and it was all gone. That touched me, and I told them so. I want all of us to love the things we own. Think of the items in your closet as puzzle pieces that, when put together, can help you convey all the complex facets of your identity. Instead of feeling like *I could take it or leave it*, I want to encourage all of us to dress in a way that makes us feel incredible. When you set an intention to feel more confident, slowly—or sometimes immediately!—you become more confident. When you dress in a way that makes you feel amazing, you start to feel, well, actually pretty amazing.

After all, looking in the mirror is a magic trick. It's the little front tuck or the perfect belt, the way you knot your sweater over your shoulders or leave your collar just peeking out that creates a feeling—when you see yourself, even you are surprised how great it looks. That said, another essentially magical aspect of style is that it's constantly growing and changing. By the time this book reaches you, my Three Words may be different. Fashion encourages evolution—and it's powerful. Once you feel steady in your style, it can take you to new places. When we allow color and the sensual feel of fabrics to touch our senses, our daring grows.

I've packed a lot into these chapters—my AB Closet-Editing System and Three-Word Method. We've covered the Nine Universal pieces, Bases, and Formulas. We've explored rituals to banish judgment and embrace authenticity. We've discussed new ways of shopping, and dressing, with care and consideration.

Most importantly, when you read this book I want you to realize that you already have good style. I hope that the tools and methods I have shared make you feel more joyful and at ease while getting dressed, but also more deeply *you*. I hope I've given you a framework for seeing your wardrobe as a cohesive and lively space of invention. Some of my favorite moments in my work with clients happen when they realize that they have everything they need. This book is designed to help you decipher and rediscover what's already in your closet and to help you find the fun in refining your look. We are all so privileged to have this chance to indulge our desires and visions by dressing ourselves. Why not enjoy every second of the process and hope that it spills over, inspiring the people around you?

And the time is now. We all want to put things off. I've heard clients say, "I'll work on my wardrobe when I've lost weight," or "I'll focus on my clothes when I have more money." Feeling fluid while expressing yourself takes some practice, and this process is about deserving self-care and nice things while working with what you've got, not waiting until you feel more worthy. I have clients who hoard amazing clothes that they never wear because they haven't found a special enough occasion. But I propose that we make every day special. Wear it just because you like it, because it makes you feel good. Life is too short! So, if you are someone who is waiting for a special moment to feel good, even better—let's make it happen today.

ACKNOWLEDGMENTS

There are so many people who made this book possible. First and foremost, my clients—you have taught me so much. So much of what I share in this book I learned by working with all of you, which is such an incredible privilege, whether we connect via a FaceTime session or an Instagram DM. Thank you for all of your feedback and wisdom! Thanks to my mom for being so supportive and never questioning my fashion choices (at least not to my face!), which always gave me the confidence to try new things. I am so grateful for you. And thanks to my dad. Some would be shocked to know that you're my social media secret weapon. You have amazing ideas, and I love brainstorming with you. You are so supportive, and when I hear you tell people about me and my job, it is one of the most heartwarming things in the world. You are the only person who has compared being a stylist with being a doctor, explaining that we both meet people at parties who want to show us their rash—or their shoes—and that both stylists and doctors make people feel better. It's a stretch, but so kind. To Mark—you were my first styling client when we were both small, and you continue to be such a good sport. I am proud to be your sister. To Nathan, thank you for pushing me and giving me such incredible ideas. I'm very lucky to have a husband who is also a manager. Your support and encouragement mean everything to me. And for the rest of my family—thank you for all of your support and inspiration. It feels unfair that I get to have all of you.

For Emily, thank you for listening to my client stories and suggesting that I write this book in the first place. You made me understand that while everyone's story is unique, we all just want to feel good. I hope that we can all see ourselves in these stories. To Delphine, thank you for suggesting that I start offering fashion tips on my Instagram all those years ago, which was the catalyst for all the rest. You're so creative and smart, and you always force me to push the boundaries. You give me confidence, and you're also the only one who will tell me if I should refilm because my hair is doing something weird. I wouldn't be able to do anything that I do without your support and guidance. For Violette . . . Honestly, none of this would be without you and your encouragement. The opportunities you have given me have been unparalleled. I would still be afraid to show my face on camera if it wasn't for you. Watching the way you navigate your business has given me a road map. I am forever grateful to you.

Thank you, Jessica, for helping me transform my rambling ideas into fully formed concepts. You have been so helpful and such a good sounding board for me through the process. I would not have been able to do this without you, and I wouldn't want to. Meg—thank you for being such an ally and teacher throughout this process. It was all very new to me and you helped me navigate publishing and didn't flinch when I asked questions that I'm sure seemed incredibly obvious. To Cara and the entire Chronicle publishing team—thank you for understanding my vision and helping push me to create something I am proud of!

Thank you to Jen Trahan for the incredible photography. It was so freeing to have someone with your eye to work on this with me. Dana Boyer, thank you for making me feel beautiful and confident. I also want to thank Jag Models and Lily Grace for helping me coordinate these amazing muses. Thank you to Selena, Omega, Kelia, Mnatalla, and Joy—you were all so fun and brought your own style that inspired me! Thank you, Lauren Sands, for so generously letting us use your incredible closet!

Thank you, Annie, for the incredible collages! Follow her at @anniecollage!

To my friends, I love you all. I am so lucky to have such a great support system.

Thank you, Aubrey, for all of your help. I wouldn't be able to do it without you.

Also, much appreciation for Christian Allaire (*Vogue*), Kristen Nichols (Who What Wear), Halie LeSavage (*Harper's Bazaar*), Jessica Testa (*New York Times*), Olivia Luppino (*The Cut*), and all of the other amazing journalists who were so kind and supportive to write about my FaceTime sessions and TikToks. Your press and encouragement were everything.

Thank you, Deewee. I miss you.

Acknowledgments

ABOUT THE AUTHOR

ALLISON BORNSTEIN is a stylist and wardrobe consultant who specializes in helping "everyday" people look and feel fantastic. She found her passion during the pandemic by helping women from all over the world find their personal style and curate their closets via FaceTime. Allison hopes to empower people to view fashion as a tool for self-expression and overall wellness. By encouraging her clients to shop their closets, tune in to their authentic needs, and embrace the pleasure of "repeat dressing," Allison has created a brand that is as much about sustainability as it is about joy. You can learn more about her work at allisonbornstein.com, on Instagram @allisonbornstein6, on TikTok @allisonbornstein6, and on YouTube. She splits her time between New York and LA.